AMERICAN MONEY MANAGEMENT, LLC

SEC Registered Investment Advisor

www.amminvest.com

Our 5 Core Investment Principles

1. Asset allocation is the most important decision

The decision of how much to invest in broad asset classes is the determining factor in your portfolio's variation and return. Your asset allocation target will be based on your financial condition, goals, and risk tolerance.

2. The price you pay determines your return

The lower the price paid for an investment, the higher your expected return, all else being equal. We take an active approach to investing, and we seek to buy only at prices that make economic sense.

3. Volatility is not risk

Real risk is the likelihood of permanent capital loss. When constructing portfolios, we focus less on the risk of investment fluctuation (a near constant in investing) and more on the potential for capital impairment.

4. Time is your ally, but returns are not linear

Research and history show that it is over the long term that investors have the best opportunity to secure the returns they need. We refuse to be swayed by market hype and fear, instead maintaining our focus on generating long-term returns.

5. No one can predict the future

No matter how hard investors and forecasters try, the future will forever be unknowable. The good news is that a crystal ball is not necessary to achieve investment success, as long as we remain focused on Principles 1–4.

About

The AMM Dividend Letter is a monthly email newsletter that is sent to the clients of American Money Management LLC, an SEC registered investment advisor. Each letter discusses a position currently held within the AMM Dividend Growth Portfolio: its potential dividend growth, the catalysts for price appreciation and dividend growth, the risks to our investment, and an estimate of its fair value.

The AMM Dividend Growth Portfolio is an active strategy. Companies discussed in the following book may no longer be a part of the portfolio. Where applicable we include our Portfolio Update Letters when a position is sold or bought out and is no longer a position in the AMM Dividend Growth Portfolio. Some positions were bought out or sold before we had a chance to write about them.

AMM Dividend Letter Volume 3 contains issues 25 through 31 sent between January 2016 and December 2016.

American Money Management LLC.

14249 Rancho Santa Fe Farms. Rd.

Rancho Santa Fe, CA. 92067

Mailing address:

PO Box 675203

Rancho Santa, Fe, CA. 92067

Tel: (858)755-0909

Email: info@amminvest.com

Table of Contents

Why Dividend Growth Investing?

Dividend growth investing is a stock investment strategy focused on total returns with a major emphasis on producing a rising income stream.

A stock can generate returns for investors primarily in two ways. A stock can increase in price and it can pay its shareholders a dividend.

Dividend Growth investing is the process of finding a stock that should increase in price and more importantly grow their dividend at above average rates year-in and year-out.

What is a Dividend?

A dividend is a regular payment of money out of profits from a company to its shareholders. U.S. publicly traded companies usually pay a quarterly dividend. Foreign companies listed in the U.S. as ADRs (American Depository Receipts) typically pay a semi-annual dividend with the end of year dividend being the larger payment.

Dividends are also a way for investors to extract value from their investment without having to sell their shares. The company returns the excess cash flow that they cannot use back to its owners, the shareholders, in the form of a dividend.

A dividend is also proof that a company is generating cash. The earnings that publicly traded companies report are easy to massage or engineer, dividends are not.

Lower Volatility

Volatility is basically the day-to-day price fluctuations of a stock.

Disciplined companies that reward their shareholders with a consistently growing dividend are in-turn rewarded with loyal shareholders. These shareholders are less likely to sell their stock based on a short-term earnings disappointment, unflattering headlines, or a general stock market correction. Loyal dividend growth investors are also more inclined to buy more stock when the price is down. They are taking advantage of the lower price to build their income stream.

Inflation Protection

Inflation the rising price of goods and services, is one the biggest risks to your income. It silently erodes the purchasing power of your money.

Investing in dividend growth stocks is a great strategy to fight the effects of inflation. Companies that pay a regularly growing dividend are usually industry leaders with pricing power. They can raise the prices on their goods and services to exceed inflation.

This pricing power combined with high operational efficiency allows these companies to raise their dividend, your income, far faster than inflation. Not only do dividend growth companies protect your purchasing power but they increase it over time.

The AMM Dividend Growth Portfolio

Dividend oriented investors often focus too much on current yield (i.e. how much the company pays the investor today), which, by extension, leads to a portfolio of mature slower growth businesses like regulated utilities or telecommunications service companies. These companies may offer relatively high current yields, yet their growth prospects are low. We aren't against investing in these industries; however, we don't think an investor seeking long-term wealth creation should necessarily overweight their portfolio in these kinds of businesses.

When we developed the AMM Dividend Strategy we decided to focus on overcoming the current yield dilemma (high payout, low growth) in dividend investing. To build a more growth oriented dividend portfolio we focus on three core types of dividend payers as the building blocks of our portfolios.

Dividend Stalwarts

Companies that have strong dependable market positions, that pay a reasonable dividend (~2-3%), and have shown an ability to grow their dividends over a long period of time at a pace far faster than inflation. While the current yield is modest, we expect the growth in the dividend payout to provide a more robust yield (on original cost) in the future.

Restructuring/Special Situations

Companies undergoing a restructuring, spin-off, or other special situation. Usually this involves a parent company spinning off a business to its existing shareholders. If we see value in the restructuring and the parent company pays a reasonable dividend we will invest. Our initial time frame for these investments is one year but if, after the restructuring, one of the companies' appears to offer good odds of becoming a Dividend Stalwart we may hold our investment for a longer time frame.

New Dividend Payers

Companies that have recently initiated a dividend policy. While these companies do not have the long history of paying and growing their dividend like the stalwarts, they do have a strong market position and the cash flow to become a stalwart in the future.

New Dividend payers tend to start their dividend at a low payout ratio (Dividends ÷ Total Earnings). As management and the board become more comfortable with paying a dividend, they tend to increase their dividend at above average rates. Whereas as Dividend Stalwarts grow their dividends at high single digit rates, we expect New Dividend Payers to grow their dividends between 10-20%.

Concentrated Portfolio

The AMM Dividend Growth Portfolio will own a maximum of 27 individual positions. The majority of the portfolio 60-70% will be invested in Dividend Stalwarts. 20-30% will be invested in New Dividend Payers. 10-20% will be invested in Special Situations. These percentages are not hard rules. The amount invested in each category will fluctuate based on the available opportunities.

Even with the concentrated nature of the portfolio, we target a low turnover ratio. We do not want to trade in and out of securities because excess trading produces excess fees and tends to lead to poor performance.

The following collection of AMM Dividend letters will further explain our investment philosophy, investment process, and portfolio construction.

Issue 25: Year in Review

January 2016

Making Predictions & Thinking Probabilistically

Predictions. We humans love listening to, making, and trusting predictions. Since it's the start of a new year we're going to be inundated with a lot of predictions about the year to come. The thing is we are really bad at making predictions; especially stock market predictions.

The chart below, from Morgan Housel's The Blind Forecaster, shows the average Wall Street strategist's forecast for S&P 500 returns each year compared to the actual gain/loss in the S&P 500 for that year since 2000.

Chart courtesy of the Fool.com.

According to Morgan Housel, the average Wall Street strategist was off by 14.7 percentage points a year! And these guys and gals get paid the big bucks.

What if you simply took the S&P 500's long-term average return of about 9% and used that as your guess? Morgan Housel took a look at this too and this strategy beat the pros, but you still would have been very wrong. Your forecasts would've been off by 14.1 percentage points per year.

Dynamic System

Why is it so hard to make stock market forecasts? It seems fairly easy right. Get a reasonable estimate of earnings for 2016, apply a basic multiple, and voila you have the S&P 500 target price and the return for the year. It's that easy!

Not quite. The stock market is a dynamic system. It is an interplay between millions of moving parts and participants. Like the weather, another dynamic system, each little change ripples throughout the system causing large and unforeseen effects rendering predictions useless.

It's the butterfly effect; a butterfly flapping its wing in some far off place causes a hurricane. Or to put it another more official way.

> In chaos theory, the butterfly effect is the sensitive dependence on initial conditions in which a small change in one state of a deterministic nonlinear system can result in large differences in a later state.

Always Know Your Base Rate

If we're planning a trip to San Diego 6 months from now we don't need to know exactly what the weather will be like. We can reasonably expect the weather to be sunny and about 71 degrees Fahrenheit, the average June climate in San Diego. We can make this reasonable assumption because we have centuries of weather data that we can average. This is called the Base Rate.

The long-term average return of the S&P 500 is a reasonable base rate for stock market returns. Once an investor knows the base rate, they should then determine whether they have any special knowledge to adjust the base rate up or down to make a better prediction. Given the poor track record of Wall Street strategists who are literally paid to make these predictions, we should assume we have no special knowledge. In this case, all investors should simply use the base rate.

We don't need to come up with a better prediction than the long-term average returns for the equity markets. We're not trying to get in and out of the stock market at just the right time. Because the markets are dynamic systems, a decision to sell one day will look completely foolish the next. All the buying and selling leads to more transactional fees, a guaranteed loss of your money.

Think Probabilistically

We also enter 2016 knowing that the market will not likely return its exact average (i.e. the base rate) for the year. It rarely ever does as the chart below shows.

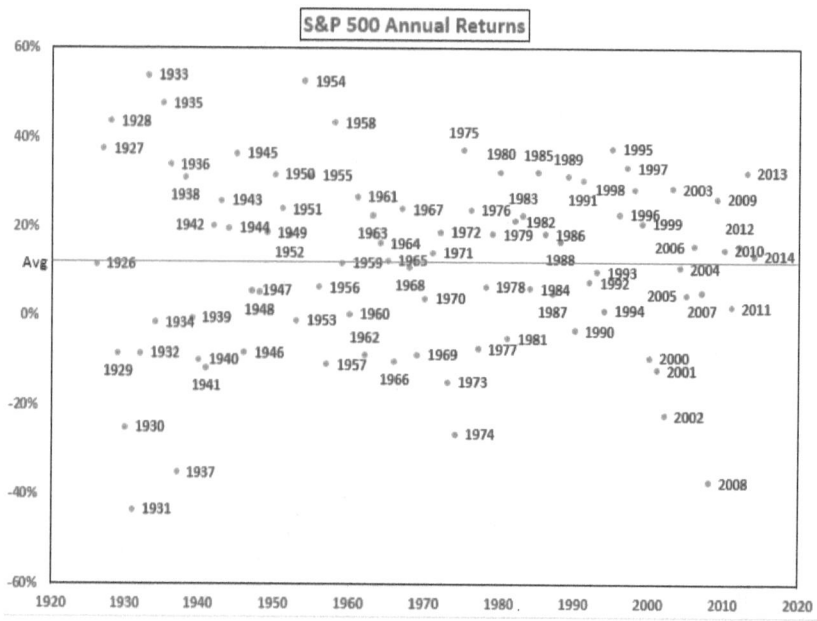

Chart courtesy of A Wealth of Common Sense.

The other big issue with market predictions, and maybe why investors are inclined to trust them so much, is that the people who make them are typically both confident and very specific. In fact as the data show, the forecasters are terribly overconfident in their ability to make predictions. In dynamic systems like the stock market, it is better to think probabilistically with a range of potential outcomes as opposed to trying to predict a single outcome.

To be as confident as the other market prognosticators, we want our range of outcomes to fall within the 95% confidence interval. The following is our prediction of probable returns for the S&P 500 in 2016. Feel free to use this prediction to wow your friends with your clairvoyance.

The S&P 500 will return between **-25% and +25%!**

And you wonder why CNBC has not called us to appear on TV yet.

How is This Useful?

What can anyone do with this prediction?

While the range we give is wide the actual skew of the distribution curve is shifted more towards positive returns. Even though no one knows what the stock market will do each year the odds favor positive returns and, over longer time periods (10-30+ years), the odds greatly favor positive returns. Also, the longer the time period the tighter the range of probable return outcomes with a clear shift towards more positive outcomes.

The Stock Market's Positive Returns: 1871-2014

Through holding periods of 15 years or greater, the stock market's total returns, including reinvested dividends, have always been positive. For five- and 10-year intervals, there have been periods of loss, but these have been infrequent.

	5-year	10-year	15-Year	20-year	30-year
Stocks	15.8%	8.5%	5.2%	10.2%	11.3%
Updated Equity Data	5-year	10-year	15-year	20-year	30-year
Best	27.0%	19.0%	17.8%	16.9%	13.8%
25th Percentile	14.9	13.2	12.0	11.6	10.8
Median	9.5	8.6	8.4	8.2	9.6
75th Percentile	3.3	5.4	6.1	6.7	6.9
Worst	-15.6	-2.1	0.2	2.8	4.1
	5-year	10-year	15-Year	20-year	30-year
Number of times negative	16	4	0	0	0
Number of times total	139	134	129	124	114

Note: Data as of 12/31/14. The 25th, Median, and 75th numbers are break points for the returns and not specific years.

Source: WisdomTree Asset Management

Image courtesy of Barrons.

And that's what you do. You make a plan to save and invest for a long period of time, 10+ years, and then stick to the plan. You avoid the Siren's call to trade around yearly market predictions. It is the best way to keep the odds ever in your favor.

Happy New Year!

Your Portfolio Management Team

Novartis (NVS) from Issue 13

Novartis is a large well-diversified pharmaceutical company. It operates in branded pharmaceuticals, generic pharmaceuticals, eye care, and consumer health.

Novartis' branded drug divisions had its heart failure drug, LCZ696, approved in the U.S. and EU and officially named Entresto. Sales are off to a strong start and peak sales are expected to top $5 billion. Cosentyx, an immunology drug, was also recently approved and its peak sales are expected to reach $2 billion.

Sandoz is Novartis' generic drug division. It is one of the biggest generic businesses in the world and will receive a boost from the billions of dollars' worth of branded drugs losing their patents over the next 5-10 years. Part of this growth will come from the new and developing biosimilar market, "generic" versions of biologics, e.g. Amgen's Neupogen, have gone off patent and generic drug companies like Sandoz are selling their cheaper versions.

At the current price around $84 per share the market is undervaluing the potential of Novartis' branded drug pipeline, generic drug opportunities, and the return of growth to its eye care division, Alcon.

BlackRock Inc. (BLK) from Issue 14

From December 1, 2015 to December 14, 2015 BlackRock (BLK) lost about 11% of its market cap. During this time, another famous asset manager Third Avenue Management had to shut down its Focused Credit Fund (TFCIX) because of mounting withdrawals and the lack of liquidity in the junk bond market. BlackRock runs one of the largest junk bond ETFs (JNK). Never missing a chance to throw the baby out with the bathwater, BlackRock shares sold off even though JNK represents only 0.22% of BlackRock's total AUM. To be fair, whatever affects the overall bond and equity markets affects all of BlackRock's business but to be hyper-concerned about one ETF is too narrow of a focus.

BlackRock is the world's largest asset manager and is well balanced between fixed-income and equities, including both active and passive strategies. We expect short-term market gyrations and fears to present more opportunities to add to our position in BlackRock.

Issue 15 was the 2014 yearend review

General Electric (GE) from Issue 16

General Electric had a busy year. It jumped through all of the regulatory hoops to buy French company Alstom's power business. GE had a deal to sell its appliance business to Electrolux only to have U.S. anti-trust regulators nix the deal. CEO Jeff Immelt says he expects to find another buyer at the start of 2016.

In 2015, GE finalized the spin-off of Synchrony Financial. We were hoping to get GE's remaining 85% stake spun-off directly to current shareholders, but that didn't happen. GE did an exchange offering whereby it offered to sell SYF shares to current GE shareholders at a 7% market discount. Then GE would use the cash raised to buy back more of its own shares, about 7% of its then shares outstanding. We declined to participate in the offering. We wanted to maintain our complete position in GE to participate further in its restructuring and plans for returning more capital to shareholders.

GE sold its commercial lending and leasing business, the last big chunk of GE Capital, with $32 billion in assets to Wells Fargo. The bulk of the proceeds from the sale will go to returning capital to shareholders.

Finally, GE received a boost when activist investor Nelson Peltz and his Trian Fund announced they owned 1% of GE. Mr. Peltz then publically said they are in agreement with everything Jeff Immelt is doing and their new stake is not an activist stake.

Norfolk Southern (NSC) from Issue 17

When we discussed Norfolk Southern we mentioned that the failed merger of Canadian Pacific (CP) and CSX (CSX) opened the door for Norfolk Southern to be involved in a deal. Then in early November Canadian Pacific announced that they would like to buy Norfolk Southern in a $28.4 billion deal. NSC rejected the offer because it did not "fairly value" the company and NSC management does not think the deal will pass anti-trust regulation. Canadian Pacific revised its offer on December 16, 2015, to include a bonus payment of up to $3.4 Billion to NSC shareholders if the combined company's shares are not worth $175 by October 2017.

Then the CEO of Berkshire Hathaway owned BNSF made the statement that they would be interested in making a competing offer for NSC. There are so few Class 1 railroads left that if the industry begins another round of consolidation then all operators have to get involved.

Finding the right dollar amount or the right bidder to get the deal done are not the biggest issues. Given the high level of concentration in the industry the railroad operators face large anti-trust/regulatory hurdles to any prospective merger. While we think the optimum number of Class 1 operators is two, we don't think there is a high probability that the regulators will see it that way.

If/when NSC is bought it will take a long time for the deal to consummate (likely a year at minimum). In the meantime, we will continue to buy NSC below our estimate of fair value and wait to see what happens with any potential merger deals.

PayChex (PAYX) from Issue 18

The big news for PayChex is that the Federal Reserve raised short-term inerest rates. PayChex's payroll processing service takes control of its clients' funds before distributing it out to its clients' employees. Like insurance companies these funds become float or cash in PayChex's accounts that it can earn interest on. Unlike insurance companies that can invest their float for long periods of time because their liabilities are many years into the future, PayChex's float is extremely short-term. PayChex has to balance the ability to earn interest on their float with the short-term liabilities of their Clients' payroll. PayChex does this by buying short-term paper like 1-3 year U.S. Treasuries, 1-3 year corporate bonds, and commercial paper.

Before the current low-interest rate environment, PayChex used to earn a blended yield of 4% on funds held for clients. Now that blended yield is 0.9%. Higher rates will allow PayChex to earn more interest income on funds held for clients. We don't expect to reach pre-2007 interest rates levels for some time. If the Federal Reserve continues to raise short-term rates then one of PayChex's most profitable divisions will benefit greatly.

ExxonMobil (XOM) from Issue 19

ExxonMobil is the only remaining position we have in the oil supermajors. As we highlighted, ExxonMobil has one of the lowest breakeven price points in regards to the price of oil to cover operational costs and its ability to continue to pay its dividend. ExxonMobil's revenue and income are balanced between upstream operations (exploration and production), and downstream operations (refining and marketing). ExxonMobil was even able to grow its dividend this year by 6%. The company also has room on its balance sheet to make a large acquisition of another oil company during this period of industry stress. Management has successfully done this during past oil bear markets.

ExxonMobil is the largest oil and company and its fortunes are tied to the price of oil. When oil prices rise ExxonMobil's cash flow and share price will rise with it. As long as oil prices remain low, ExxonMobil will be under pressure. Our job is to monitor ExxonMobil's financial statements for its ability to maintain its current dividend policy and ExxonMobil's ability to grow its dividend well into the future. If things change to the point that ExxonMobil cannot maintain the dividend policy then we will sell.

Philip Morris (PM) from Issue 20

Philip Morris is probably the most controversial position we own. For those clients who've requested not to own any tobacco stocks we understand your position and we have not bought Philip Morris for your account. Tobacco stocks have been unloved for a long time. It is the general disdain that has kept the price of shares in tobacco companies well below their intrinsic value. In general, tobacco companies need very little capital to grow and maintain their business. Tobacco companies also turn their inventory over so quickly that they generate high returns on invested capital and even higher returns on tangible capital. Philip Morris is no exception. The excess returns and low capital needs mean more capital can be returned to shareholders through increased dividends and share buybacks. Combined with the low price to intrinsic value equates to higher shareholder returns over time.

One of the biggest threats to Philip Morris and the other tobacco companies is plain packaging laws circulating among the world's legislators. It looks like Philip Morris and other tobacco companies will lose their challenge to the EU's top court plain packaging laws. Other countries will follow suit. Advertising and brand building allows Philip Morris to charge premium prices. When cigarette packages all look the same will Philip Morris be able to charge premium prices?

Baxter International (BAX) & Baxalta (BXLT) from Issue 21

As soon as the spin-off of Baxalta from Baxter occurred both companies experienced positive catalysts. Activist Investor Dan Loeb of Third Point took a 10% stake in the new Baxter (BAX). Mr. Loeb and his investment firm sought and received a position on the company's board and a role in bringing in a new CEO. The new CEO, Jose Almeida, is a proven deal maker. He became CEO of Covidien in 2011 and built a truly global company through a series of acquisitions and growth initiatives. Then Mr. Almeida sold Covidien to Medtronic for $49 Billion in 2014.

Baxalta upon separation from Baxter immediately received a $30.6 Billion buyout offer from Shire Plc. Baxalta rebuffed the offer stating it was too low and that they had no interest in doing a deal. Shire Plc maintained their interest and the persistence paid off as management from Baxalta and Shire met recently to discuss terms. Because of Baxalta's recent spin-off and to maintain its tax-free status the deal will involve a mix of Shire shares and cash. With more shares than cash. If/when a final deal is announced we'll decide whether we want to maintain our position in the new company or sell our position.

Union Pacific (UNP) from Issue 22

The concerns facing Union Pacific are: slowing economy/recession, lower oil prices, and lower commodity prices. We made our first purchase of UNP in the face of these headwinds and the environment is still the same. Railroads remain the most efficient way to move goods over long distances within the U.S. Short-term economic fluctuations will weigh on UNP's stock price. However, in the long-run we expect the U.S. economy and global economy to continue to grow and railroads will be there to transport the goods.

Johnson & Johnson (JNJ) from Issue 23

Nothing new to report since we first wrote about Johnson & Johnson. An acquisition of a biotech company is still a possibility with valuations of potential targets still coming down. If Johnson & Johnson does not make an acquisition in the coming year we would like to see a more aggressive return of capital to shareholders. Interest rates are still extremely low and JNJ has the room on their balance sheet to take on more debt to finance aggressive share buybacks and/or a special dividend to shareholders.

The Walt Disney Co. (DIS) from Volume 24

Disney was the subject of our most recent letter so there is nothing new to report. Except that Star Wars VII: The Force Awakens is destroying box office records as if they were a Death Star getting proton torpedoes sent into its thermal exhaust port by a rebel X-Wing fighter.

Issue 26: Yum! Brands (YUM)

February 2016

What Does the Market Know?

We like to think we do a decent job of writing these letters; however we're realists and we do not hold illusions of grandeur that we are the Hemingway of financial writing. One investor that may be vying for this title is Howard Marks. Mr. Marks is the Chairman of Oaktree Capital and has been writing his memos for Oaktree investors since the early 90s. Howard's memos have become a must-read within the finance industry. Warren Buffet says it's the first thing he reads whenever a new memo is released.

The latest memo talks about "The Market". We commonly look at the broad equity market and assign an intelligence to it especially during times of stress. We think the market "knows" something that we don't. It doesn't.

> So, what does the market know? **First it's important to understand for this purpose that there really isn't such a thing as "the market." There's just a bunch of people who participate in a market**. The market isn't more than the sum of the participants, and it doesn't "know" any more than their collective knowledge.
>
> This is a very important point. If you believe the market has some special insight that exceeds the collective insight of its participants, then you and I have a fundamental disagreement. The thinking of the crowd isn't synergistic. In my view, the investment IQ of the market isn't any higher than the average IQ of the participants. And everyone who transacts gets a volume-weighted vote in setting an asset's price at a given point in time.
>
> People of all different levels of ability act together to set the price. They vary all over the lot in terms of knowledge, experience, insight and emotionalism. The market doesn't give the ones who are superior in these regards any more influence than the others, especially in the short run. **My bottom line on this subject is that the market price merely reflects the average insight of the market participants**. That's point number one.

If anything, I think it's emotion that's synergistic. It builds into herd behavior or mass hysteria. When 10,000 people panic, the emotion seems to snowball. People influence each other, and their emotions compound, so that the overall level of panic in the market can be higher than the panic of any participant in isolation. That's something I'll return to later.

Now let's think about the first goal of investing: to buy low. We want to buy things whose price underestimates the value of the underlying assets or earnings (value investing) or the future potential (growth investing). **In either case, we're looking for instances when the market is wrong**. If we thought the market was always right – the efficient market hypothesis – we wouldn't spend our lives as active investors. Since we do, we'd better believe we know more than the consensus. **So by definition we must not think the market – that is, the sum of all other investors – knows everything, or knows more than we do, or is always right**. That's point number two.

And that leads logically to point number three: why take instruction from a group of people who know less than you do? In "On the Couch," I wrote that it all seems obvious: investors rarely maintain objective, rational, neutral and stable positions. Do you agree with that or not? Is the market a clinical and rational fundamental analyst, or a barometer of investor sentiment? Does the market's behavior these days look like something a mature adult should emulate?

It seems clear to me: the market does not have above average insight, but it often is above average in emotionality. Thus we shouldn't follow its dictates. In fact, contrarianism is built on the premise that we generally should do the opposite of what the crowd is doing, especially at the extremes, and I prefer it.

Large price swings in assets do not indicate a market intelligence. What it does show is the current state of investor psychology.

Fundamentals – the outlook for an economy, company or asset – don't change much from day to day. **As a result, daily price changes are mostly about (a) changes in market psychology and thus (b) changes in who wants to own something or un-own something.** These two statements become increasingly valid the more daily prices fluctuate. Big fluctuations show that psychology is changing radically.

And, I said on page two, emotional fluctuations – swings in market sentiment or psychology – do seem to be synergistic. That is, in crowd psychology, 2 + 2 = 5. **While I don't think the price of an asset reflects more wisdom than is possessed by the average of its market's members, I do believe mass psychology will make a group swing to reach greater emotional extremes than its members would separately.** In short, people make each other crazy. And when times are bad – like now – they depress each other. That was a factor in the edge enjoyed by our distressed debt team in 2008: they were able to buy at the market's lows because they weren't in New York, where everyone was trading scary stories and getting each other down.

Again, we can gain insight through logic. **We all know we want to buy (not sell) at the lows, and sell (not buy) at the highs. So then how can it be right to sell because of a decline or buy because of a rise?** Advocates of this latter approach must think (a) declines and rises tend to continue more than they reverse and/or (b) they can tell which declines mean "buy" and which mean "sell." Some savants may have that latter ability, but not many. In general, I think it's ridiculous to sell something because it's down (just as it is to buy because it's up).

We shouldn't be basing our decisions on what the market is doing.

So the bottom-line question is simple: does the market reflect what people know, or should people base their actions on what the market knows? And if the latter, where does "the market" get its information, other than from people? For me it's simple: if people follow the market's dictates, they're taking advice from . . . themselves!

Read the whole memo, it's worth it.

Sincerely,

Your Portfolio Management Team

Dividend Stock in Focus

YUM! Brands (YUM): $69

Prices as of the close February 11, 2016

When we developed the AMM Dividend Strategy we decided to focus on dividend growth over high current dividend yield investing. We focus on three core types of dividend payers as the building blocks of our dividend strategy portfolios.

1) Dividend Stalwarts: Companies that have strong dependable market positions, that pay a reasonable dividend (~2-3%), and have shown an ability to grow their dividends over a long period of time at a pace far faster than inflation. While the current yield is modest, we expect the growth in the dividend payout to provide a more robust yield (on original cost) in the future.

2) Restructuring/Special Situations: Companies undergoing a restructuring, spin-off, or other special situation. If we see value in the restructuring and the parent company pays a reasonable dividend we will invest. Our initial time frame for these investments is one year but if, after the restructuring, one of the companies' appears to offer good odds of becoming a dividend stalwart we may hold our investment for a longer time frame.

3) New Dividend Payers: Companies that have recently initiated a dividend policy. While these companies do not have the long history of paying and growing their dividend like the stalwarts, they do have a strong market position and the cash flow to become a stalwart in the future.

Yum! Brands could easily fit into the dividend stalwart category but we've started a position in Yum! because it is undergoing a corporate restructuring. Yum! Brands is splitting into two companies. One company will focus solely on the Chinese market, Yum! China. The other company will retain all other markets with North America being the biggest one. Each new company will have a different growth and operational profile and the upcoming restructuring should unlock the value of each business.

Yum! Brands is known for owning and operating KFC, Taco Bell, and Pizza Hut. Yum! Brands itself is the result of a corporate restructuring, a spin-off, from Pepsi Co. in 1997.

Dividend History

Yum! Brands started paying a quarterly dividend in 2004. Over the last 9 years, Yum! has grown their dividend at a compound annual rate of 21%.

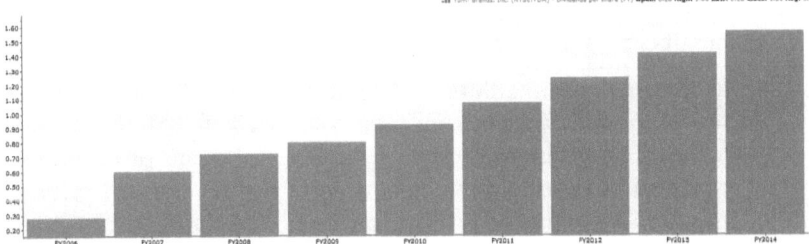

From S&P Capital IQ.

Yum! Also recently raised its dividend another 17%. The upcoming corporate restructuring should boost Yum! Brands' dividend further and potentially provide a one-time special dividend too. Yum! Brands' current payout ratio looks high at 78% but this is because of special one-time write-downs tied to recent food scandals. Yum! Brands' dividend is well covered by Free Cash Flow when we add back the one-time non-cash write-downs.

Catalysts for Dividend Growth & Capital Appreciation

Spin-Off

Yum! Brands is essentially two restaurant business models combined as one. The first model is an asset-light model that relies heavily on franchising its stores and collecting royalties from the franchisees. This first model represents Yum! Brands' U.S business. The asset-light model produces lower revenue per store but generates higher margins and profitability per store.

The second model is an asset-heavy model that relies on owning and operating its stores. Yum! generates more revenue per store but controlling and operating the store is less profitable than franchising it. This model represents Yum! Brands' Chinese division. Yum! Brands has a total of 6,867 stores in China and Yum! operates 5,521 of them. Currently Yum! Brands' China division generates pre-tax operating profit margins of 10.28% while the US franchised focus division generates pre-tax operating profit margins of 23.76%.

Yum! Brands is also a combination of two different growth prospects. Yum! Brands' US division is a mature business focused on slower growth and incremental operational efficiencies. Yum! China is still an emerging business and a play on the growth of the Chinese middle class. Management believes they can build out 20,000 stores in China.

> Yum! China has the **potential to grow to 20,000 restaurants or more in the future from approximately 6,900 restaurants today**. The business also has significant sales and profit growth potential in its existing restaurants, which the Company plans to capture over time by growing its core offerings and expanding further into new initiatives such as home delivery. – From 8K released 10-20-2015

Separating the two business models and two growth prospects from each other should unlock the hidden value of the two businesses.

Yum! China

The table below highlights a few US Companies that we think are comparable companies to Yum! China. While we think of KFC and Pizza Hut as traditional fast-food companies in the U.S., in China these brands are viewed more like traditional casual restaurants. U.S. casual restaurant companies like Brinker (EAT), DineEquity (DIN), and Darden Restaurants (DRI) own and operate their restaurants like Yum! China.

Once Yum! China is spun-off from Yum! Brands it will trade on US exchanges. We will use these companies as comparables to estimate a range of potential values for Yum! China.

Company Comp Set	
Company Name	TEV/EBIT LTM - Latest
Chipotle Mexican Grill, Inc. (NYSE:CMG)	16.0x
Red Robin Gourmet Burgers Inc. (NasdaqGS:RRGB)	14.4x
Darden Restaurants, Inc. (NYSE:DRI)	14.2x
Noodles & Company (NasdaqGS:NDLS)	24.8x
Shake Shack Inc. (NYSE:SHAK)	28.3x
Brinker International, Inc. (NYSE:EAT)	12.3x
DineEquity, Inc. (NYSE:DIN)	12.9x
Yum! Brands, Inc. (NYSE:YUM)	15.1x

Data from S&P Capital IQ.

Yum! China added 448 net new stores for the period ending September 5, 2015, for a total unit count of 6,867.

Unit Count	9/5/2015	9/6/2014
Company-owned	5,521	5,158
Unconsolidated Affiliates	778	735
Franchise & License	568	526
	6,867	6,419

Over the trailing 12 months Yum! China generated revenues of $6.867 Billion which equals $1 million in sales per store. Over the same trailing 12 months Yum! China generated $693 million in operating profits. This is a 10.09% operating profit margin.

Using the highlighted companies and their multiples of 12-14x operating income, we come up with a value range of Yum! China of $8.32-9.7 Billion. This is Yum! China's estimated value today if it were trading on its own. We also want to estimate a reasonable value for Yum! China 5 years from now.

Let's say Yum! China continues to add 448 net new stores for at least the next 5 years. By 2021 Yum! China will have 9,107 stores opened. If they too can generate $1 million in sales then 2021 revenues will be $9.11 billion. At a 10% operating margin, Yum! China will generate $910.7 million in operating profit. Using the same multiples from above this produces a 5-year value range of $10.92-12.75 Billion.

Yum! China's current operating margin is under-representative of its underlying earnings power. In 2014 Yum! Brands had issues with a Chinese food supplier who was relabeling and selling meat that passed its expiration date. Expectedly Yum! Brands lowered expectations and estimates as its Chinese KFC sales fell.

Before the food scandal Yum! China had an operating margin of 14%. If Yum! China can recover from the food scare and regain operating efficiency than Yum! China is worth a lot more in 5 years. 9,107 stores producing $9.11 billion in revenue with 14% operating margins produces $1.28 billion in operating profits. Using the same 12-14x multiples produces a value range of $15.3-17.6 billion.

The multiples we're using may prove to be too conservative given Yum! China's growth prospects and potential margin expansion. The companies we used as comparables have lower growth rates and consistently produce sub 10% Operating Margins except for DineEquity (DIN).

At 10 percent operating margins we reasonably estimate that Yum! China could be worth 31% more in 5 years. If operating margins can get back to pre-scandal levels, then we estimate the company could be worth 83% more in 5 years.

It looks like Yum! China is on the right track. According to the 10Q ending September 5, 2015, Yum! China grew revenues 7 percent year-over-year and operating margins were 16% versus 11% in the period a year ago.

Yum! US

The table below includes a handful of companies that are comparable to Yum! Brands post spin-off. Outside of China & India, 91% of Yum! Brands stores are franchised. Yum! brands' goal post spin-off is to reach 95% franchised stores. The comparable companies below also have over 80% of their stores operating as franchises.

Company Comp Set	
Company Name	TEV/EBIT LTM - Latest
The Wendy's Company (NasdaqGS:WEN)	20.3x
McDonald's Corp. (NYSE:MCD)	18.1x
Jack in the Box Inc. (NasdaqGS:JACK)	16.3x
Domino's Pizza, Inc. (NYSE:DPZ)	20.6x
Papa John's International Inc. (NasdaqGS:PZZA)	16.3x
Yum! Brands, Inc. (NYSE:YUM)	16.2x

Data from S&P Capital IQ.

The higher the franchise mix, the higher the trading multiple. A post spin-off Yum! Brands with a franchise mix over 91% should trade in-line with McDonald's. For the trailing twelve months Yum! Brands generated $1.26 billion in operating profits. Applying an 18x multiple values Yum! Brands ex China at $22.7 Billion.

Yum! Brands pre-restructuring trades at a market capitalization of $31.52 Billion. At this price, we are paying a fair price for both the US and China businesses as is. However, we think Yum China! priced as it is today drastically undervalues its growth potential and its ability to rebound from its food scandal. We also think Yum! Brands' current trading price is undervaluing its US operations.

Pizza Hut

Started out as a casual dine-in pizza restaurant. The majority of pizza ordering and consumption in the U.S. has switched to delivery. Pizza Hut does deliver pizza but it still operates its casual dine-in restaurants. Pizza Hut's larger store footprint compared to delivery only options like Domino's Pizza (DPZ) leads to lower sales per square foot and lower operating margins per store. Shifting its store mix from more dine-in locations to delivery only locations will increase speed and convenience for customers and improve its operating metrics.

KFC

Compared to other chicken-focused quick service restaurants like Bojangles (BOJA) and Popeye's Louisiana Kitchen (PLKI), KFC is operating below its potential. Domestic KFC stores are profitable and growing but operations could improve. One step is modernizing their menu and increasing their exposure to chicken sandwiches, one of the fastest growing segments in fast food. Another option is expanding their hours of operation and staying open later at night. Improving the speed and quality of service is the last step.

Taco Bell

Taco Bell is Yum! Brands' best-performing segment. While it is not a fast growing segment it generates high margins and lots of free cash flow. Taco Bell's recent push into breakfast continues to drive year over year same-store-sales growth. A Taco Bell spin-off is possible. If KFC and Pizza Hut obscure the value of the Taco Bell division, we wouldn't be surprised to see activists push for a spin-off.

Recapitalization

Before the completion of the spin-off, Yum! Brands will take on more debt that will stay with Yum! Brands after the Chinese spin-off. The increased leverage is to buy back more shares and issue a special dividend before completion of the spin-off. Management plans to return about $6.2 billion to shareholders before the spin-off of Yum! China is complete.

Pre-Mortem (Potential Risks to our Thesis)

Can't Overcome Food Scandal & Operational Inefficiencies

The big question for Yum! China is if it can bounce back from its food scandal. So far we've seen positive signs. However, if the Chinese consumer is anything like the U.S. consumer it will take time to earn their trust back. It took Jack in the Box (JACK) almost 4 years to recover from its E. Coli scare.

When Yum! Brands first started operating in China it had no real local competition. Operational inefficiencies were easy to overlook as customer volume made up for it. Yum! Brands now faces more local competition and its food scandal may have pushed its former loyal customers into the arms of its competitors. The reduced customer traffic also exposed its operational inefficiencies. Not only does Yum! China need to win the trust of its customers back it also needs to improve upon its service quality and speed to keep customers happy and coming back for more.

China

China provides a great opportunity for growth but exposure here comes with commensurate risk. The biggest issue is the government itself. One day it's business friendly, and then an enemy the next. Part of the idea behind the Yum! China spin-off is to have a Chinese company that can better handle Chinese issues. I don't know how Chinese the new company will look when it will initially trade on the NYSE exclusively. A Hong Kong listing has been discussed but a timetable has not been announced. While Yum! China will be a Chinese-focused company it doesn't mean the Chinese government will recognize Yum! China as Chinese.

Another reason for the Yum! China spin-off is to create a direct play on the rise of the Chinese middle class and the country's ongoing shift to a more consumption based economy. Chinese growth has slowed in recent years, which was to be expected as the economy became larger. The question is whether or not the economy is growing much slower than officially released numbers and what this might mean for the spending habits of its burgeoning consumers. Eating out is a small luxury and an easily cut one if consumers perceive or are experiencing any economic hardship. In our opinion, a Chinese recession would be a short-term problem. However, if China's economy slowed dramatically within the next year it would be bad timing for a stand-alone Chinese focused consumer discretionary company to start trading.

Changing U.S. Consumer Tastes

The trend in quick service restaurants has been towards fast casual, "healthier" fare that tends to be locally sourced and sustainable. KFC, Taco Bell, and Pizza Hut are clearly not in this category. So far fast casual food concepts and traditional fast food outlets have coexisted and grown as more and more people eat out than make food at home. If the fast casual trend persists it will pressure sales at KFC, Taco Bell, and Pizza Hut.

Yum! Brands is well aware of the potential threat fast casual presents. Yum! launched U.S. Taco Co. as a fast casual concept restaurant, but recently shuddered the business. While Yum! is expected to launch other fast casual restaurants, the better move may be to buy an existing, emerging, and already successful brand. Given Yum! Brands increased debt load from the upcoming spin-off, any major purchase will likely require either stock issuance, which would be dilutive to current shareholders, or more debt.

Conclusion

Yum! Brands is a high-quality company that has generated high returns on equity, tangible assets, and capital for a long period of time. We've been watching it and waiting for its price to come down to a level we'd be willing to pay for the company. The Chinese food scandal created that opportunity. Food scandals are resolved quickly but the customers' perceptions persist dragging sales, earnings, and stock prices down over the short-run.

Recovering from its food scandal would have been enough of a short-term catalyst but then at the urging of an activist investor, Corvex Capital, Yum! Brands decided to spin-off its Chinese business. Our low-end fair value estimate for Yum! Brands is $88 per share and we think that value will greatly increase as both short-term catalysts come to fruition.

Issue 27: Procter & Gamble (PG)

March 2016

How to Measure Your Risk Level

Consider this proposition:

- You are offered a gamble on the toss of a coin.
- If the coin shows tails, you lose $100
- If the coin shows heads, you win $150

Is this gamble attractive? Would you accept it?

The above problem is taken from Nobel Prize winner Daniel Kahneman's book Thinking, Fast and Slow. His book has become a kind of unofficial behavioral finance bible here at AMM. As we've often said in jest, "investing isn't rocket science, it's harder". Harder, not because of the need for advanced math (a basic understanding of arithmetic is generally all that is necessary to read a financial statement), but because markets are composed of individuals who make decisions for a variety of reasons, not always rational and often driven more by sentiment and emotion than anything else.

The above proposition highlights this quandary. As Kahneman puts it, "to make this choice you must balance the psychological benefit of getting $150 against the psychological cost of losing $100. Although the expected value of the gamble is obviously positive, because you stand to gain more than you can lose, you probably dislike it – most people do. For most people the fear of losing $100 is more intense than the hope of gaining $150. We concluded from many such observations that people are loss averse."

The Loss Aversion Conundrum

Since investing is always about foregoing consumption today in the hope of having more in the future, and since the future is inherently unknowable (i.e. you may hope for more, but in fact receive less if events take a turn for the worse), then the question of risk tolerance becomes a critical component of developing an appropriate portfolio strategy. It is also important to note that risk tolerance and risk acceptance are two different beasts.

To illustrate, while stock markets have NEVER had a 20 year period of negative annualized rates of return, many investors with 20 year time horizons have sold during periods of market decline to "manage risk, stop the bleeding, lock in gains or protect the downside". So while the time horizon allowed the investor to accept the risks associated with investing in stocks, the investor's tolerance for risk caused them to sell when markets moved against them.

This might seem entirely reasonable if it weren't for the fact that this type of behavior is generally associated with poor long-term returns. A famous study on mutual fund flows from Dalbar has shown that investors are terrible timers, with fund outflows reaching their highest levels at market lows, and their highest inflows at market tops. One of our favorite drawings from BehaviorGap highlights this wealth destructive behavior.

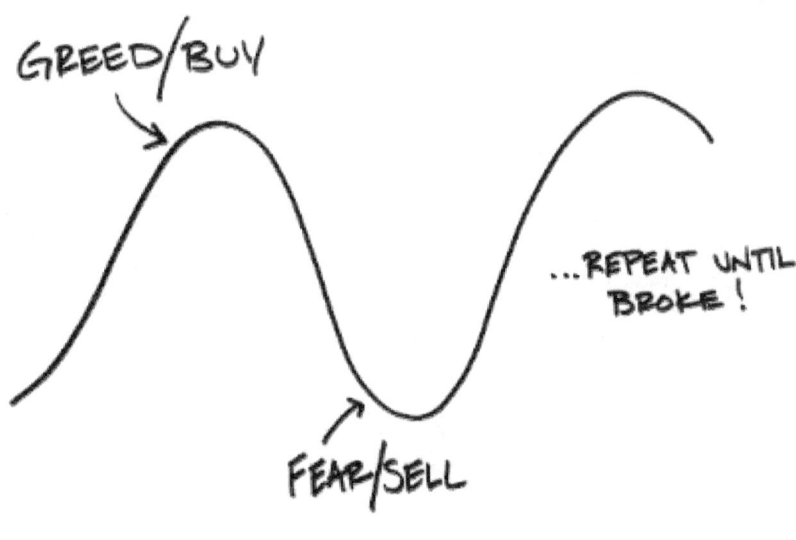

Reconciling Loss Aversion with Investing in the Real World

We know we must accept risk as part of the investment process, but we also know that we will constantly be tested by the market – feeling confident and risk tolerant when the market goes up, and insecure and risk averse when the market declines. Perhaps the most important thing for any investor to do is to accept and understand this very real psychological obstacle to their long-term investment success. Only by being cognizant of the loss aversion conundrum can one overcome it and sustain the discipline necessary to stick to their investment strategy.

We spend time at the beginning of a client relationship attempting to ascertain appropriate risk levels, generally taking into account things like time horizon, investment objectives and general tolerance for market volatility. In concert with these qualitative assessments, **we have more recently begun using a quantitative scoring system to help further our understanding of a clients' unique risk profile**.

The benefits of this approach are:

1. Incorporates real portfolio values in various win/loss propositions to develop an independent risk score
2. The risk score can be tied to actual portfolio investments to verify that your strategy is in line with your unique risk tolerance
3. The risk score can be used to help map a probability of achieving retirement/investment goals

If you haven't yet gone through this process and are interested in knowing your risk score just respond to this email and request your complimentary risk analysis.

By definition, the future will remain risky and is certain to be filled with unexpected surprises both good and bad. Just as certain, however, is that most savers need to generate a rate of return higher than the risk-free rate offered at the bank; which means they must take risk. For this reason, knowing your true risk tolerance is critical in helping you navigate both good and bad markets to ultimately achieve your investment goals.

We look forward to hearing from you!

Sincerely,

Your Portfolio Management Team

Dividend Stock in Focus

Procter & Gamble (PG): $81.78

Price as of the close March 11, 2016

William Procter was an English immigrant candle maker. James Gamble was an Irish immigrant soap maker. A little luck, both good and bad, found them both living in Cincinnati in the early 1800s.

William Procter's first wife became ill while they traveled down the Ohio River and a few months after they arrived in Cincinnati she died.

When he was 16 James Gamble and his family were headed east to Illinois. James became ill and the family had to stop in Cincinnati and eventually decided on settling there.

William Procter eventually remarried to Olivia Norris, the daughter of a local prominent candle maker. He worked at a bank and made candles on the side to help make ends meet. James Gamble, who by this time had his own soap and candle shop, married Olivia's sister, Elizabeth Norris.

Their new father-in-law, Alexander Norris, noticed that his two new son-in-laws were competing for the same resources and customers. Mr. Norris suggested the two work together. On October 31, 1837 the Procter & Gamble company was born with total assets of $7,192.24. Procter & Gamble now has over $129 billion in total assets, a market capitalization of $224 billion, and does over $72 billion in revenue a year.

Dividend History

Procter & Gamble fits into our dividend stalwart category. It has consistently paid and raised a dividend every year for many years. It is a member of the S&P Dividend Aristocrat index. To qualify a company has to have paid and raised its dividend for at least 25 years. Procter and Gamble has done so for 58 years.

Over the last 9 years, Procter & Gamble has grown their dividend at a compound annual rate of 8.14%. We're usually looking for double digit growth but we'll sacrifice a couple of extra percentage points of growth for consistent growth. If Procter and Gamble maintains 8.14% growth its dividend, your income, will double in 8 years.

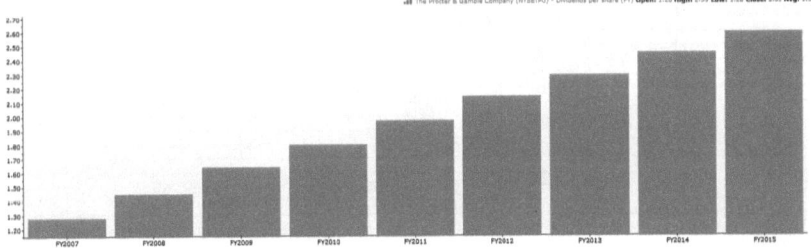

From S&P Capital IQ.

Procter & Gamble's payout ratio is currently high around 85%. Procter and Gamble recently took a one-time charge to earnings as it further undergoes its restructuring. We expect this payout ratio to drift back down towards 60% as PG finishes its plans.

Catalysts for Dividend Growth & Capital Appreciation

Divestment

Procter & Gamble got too big. It had way too many brands and it distracted the company from focusing on its fastest growing brands and its very profitable core brands. P&G has been divesting itself of 100 brands.

- Procter & Gamble sold 43 beauty brands, including CoverGirl, to Coty for $12.5 billion.
- Procter and Gamble sold its pet food business to Mars, Inc. for $2.9 billion.
- Duracell was sold to Berkshire-Hathaway in an exchange for the shares of Procter & Gamble that Berkshire-Hathaway owns.

Revenue will be lower as Procter and Gamble continues divesting itself of non-core brands. The divestment will reduce operating costs and improve profitability as the company focuses its resources on its better brands and growing them around the world.

The ultimate goal is 10 categories focusing on 65 brands.

Increasing Returns

The divestment plan is in part to improve Procter & Gamble's returns on equity, assets, and capital. Over the last 10 years, Procter & Gamble's brand bloat has reduced the returns it generates.

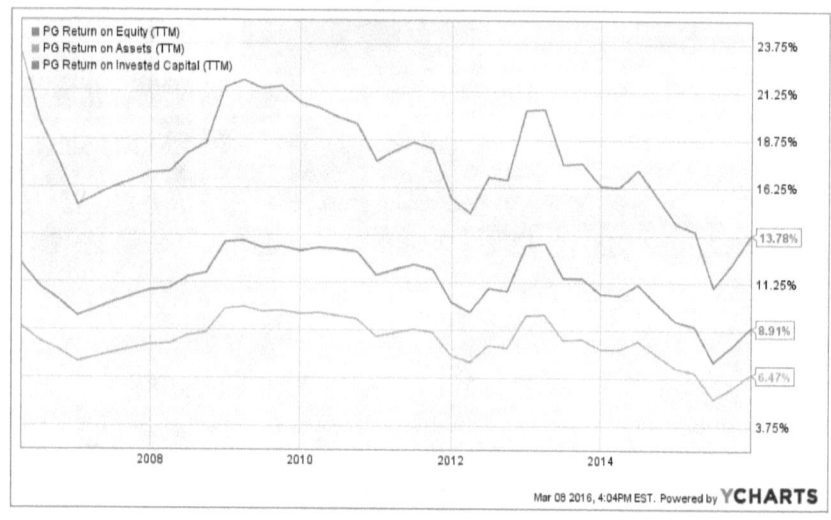

Improving the brand mix and bringing profit margins back up to old levels will increase returns and the capital it can return to shareholders.

Splitting Procter & Gamble Up

Long-term clients and readers of the AMM Dividend Letter are well aware of our love of spin-offs. We think Procter & Gamble should be split up. Spin-off benefit both the company spun-off and the parent. Both companies reduce their operating size and become more focused on their key markets. Spin-offs have been shown to increase sales and profits at both the old parent company and the new spin-off by creating the best operating environment for each.

Barron's recently outlined a 3-way split-up of Procter and Gamble and highlights the math that shows Procter & Gamble is worth more separate than together.

Too Many Moving Parts

Shareholders could see a 20% gain if P&G were broken up into three companies: beauty, health care and grooming, and home and family care.

SEGMENT	2016E Ebitda (mil)	EV / Ebitda	2016E Ent. Value (mil)
Beauty	$3,234	15.2	$49,157
Grooming	2,652	11.7	31,028
Health Care	1,899	16.2	30,764
Fabric and Home Care	4,534	17.2	77,985
Baby, Feminine, and Family Care	4,808	12.1	58,177
TOTAL COMPANY			$247,111
Enterprise value for beauty businesses being sold to Coty			14,000
Enterprise value for Duracell, being sold to Berkshire Hath.			2,200
Net Debt			-17,881
Equity Value			$245,430
Value Per Share			$90.00
Current Stock Price			$75.00
Potential Upside			20%

E=Estimate: Ebitda excludes Duracell and businesses being sold to Coty; EV/Ebitda multiples based on peer averages   Sources: Barron's; Sanford C. Bernstein; Bloomberg

Table from Barron's.

While we would like to see Procter & Gamble embark on a spin-off strategy we think this strategy is a couple years away, at least. Management has to finish their current divestment plan, corporate restructuring, and increased efficiency plans before they really consider splitting the company up.

Pre-Mortem (Potential Risks to our Thesis)

Razor Subscription Services

Procter & Gamble's highest margin business is its grooming division which houses its razor business. It was supposedly King Gillette that came up with the strategy now known as the razor/razor blade model. Sell the razor cheaply and then sell the disposable razor blade at a higher price and with high-profit margins. The story is a myth but Gillette's business model transformed into it over the years. Grooming is Procter & Gamble's highest margin division with consistent operating profit margins in excess of 30%.

High margins attract competition. In the last couple of years, two companies have taken on Procter & Gamble's razor business, Dollar Shave Club and Harry's. The cost to manufacture comparable razor blades has declined along with the cost to sell directly to consumers on a subscription basis. It allows companies like Dollar Shave Club and Harry's to sell their razors at much lower prices and accept lower margins of profitability to grab market share in a $6+ billion men's grooming market.

Private Label vs Name Brand

It's not just with razors that Procter & Gamble charges a higher price when compared to competitors. For example, Tide is the highest priced liquid detergent on the market. As the chart below from UBS via Quartz highlights.

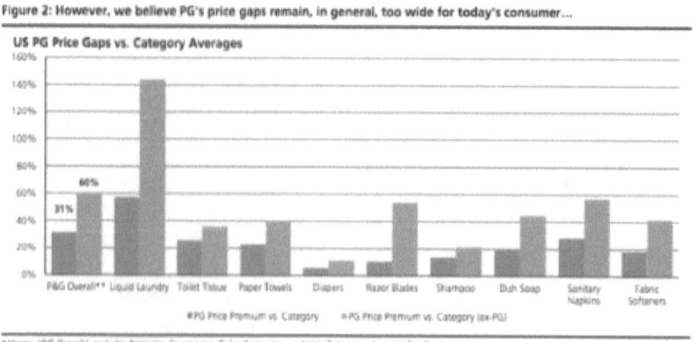

Figure 2: However, we believe PG's price gaps remain, in general, too wide for today's consumer...

Brand loyalty and pricing power were two of the main investment themes for Procter & Gamble over the years. Consumers used to be willing to pay up for name brands because of the quality the brand name implied. Brand loyalty has reversed over the years and consumers are no longer shunning private label/generic brands.

> Nearly 70% of store brand shoppers report trusting certain store brands more than others, and 64% are likely to try other store products once they've tried one. Brand trust is particularly strong for millennials, who are more likely to buy store brand foods in general (97% compared with 94% of all shoppers).

This trend dampens Procter & Gamble's ability to continue raise prices faster than the rate of inflation on its name brand products.

Emerging Markets

Why does America's leading diaper company, Procter & Gamble place a made in Japan sticker on the diapers it sells in China? Procter & Gamble misread the Chinese market. P&G believed that Chinese consumers would want value and marketed their diapers as such. Chinese parents wanted high-end diapers and the Japanese diaper maker Kao offered them. Procter & Gamble is addressing this issue with higher-end diapers that are made in Japan.

Selling a consumer good globally involves getting the branding and the value proposition correct for each market. P&G's china misstep was a big one. China is the growth market for consumer goods right now. If P&G stumbles or fails to gain a large presence in other emerging markets then its future growth will be hindered.

Conclusion

Our estimate of fair value for Procter & Gamble is $85 per share. We used current operating margins, a 4% growth rate, and a 10% discount rate. If Procter & Gamble succeeds in its divestment and restructuring plans then margins will improve and our estimate of fair value will increase. Increased revenue growth will increase our estimate of P&G's intrinsic value too.

As of right now, Procter & Gamble is fairly valued. This does not mean we expect below average returns or negative returns. It simply means at today's price we're not expecting above average returns. A lower stock price gives us a chance to buy more Procter & Gamble at a price that offers us the potential for above average returns. This is why we like stock market corrections. It is not a time to panic but a time to look for opportunity.

As we outlined above, if Procter & Gamble can achieve its restructuring operating targets while fending off threats to its core brands then P&G's intrinsic value is likely more than our current estimate.

Portfolio Update: Procter & Gamble

February 2018

We liquidated your position in Proctor and Gamble (PG) earlier this week.

While the position had generated positive total returns for our clients, dividend growth has stalled in recent years and the company is facing secular headwinds related to their core business.

Below we provide additional detail on our rationale for selling Proctor & Gamble.

Search Costs - "The Old Way"

If you're like most people you want to get in and out of the grocery store as quickly as possible. Shopping is searching for a solution to a problem or a need you have, like laundry detergent for washing your clothes.

When shopping for laundry detergent you want a product that you can trust and is guaranteed to work. You don't want to pay too much but you are willing to pay a slight premium for that trust.

There are a lot of laundry detergent brands. Before you buy you can compare each brand, their active ingredient(s), their claims of effectiveness, and price. But this would take a long time and you have 30 other items you need to shop for. You would be in the grocery store all day.

Your time is **a precious resource and it is costly to spend** all this time searching for one product.

Again, if you're like most people you grab a brand of laundry detergent that you're familiar with. You may even spend an extra $1-2 for a "name brand" because you know and trust this brand.

Consumer branded products like those that Proctor and Gamble sells have done well over the years because they lowered your search costs. It made your trip to the grocery store quicker. Your time and peace of mind are expensive so you are willing to pay a premium price for the name brand product.

Big name consumer brands were built on national print and TV advertising campaigns. They could afford it.

For years this was a virtuous circle. The more the brand spent on advertising the higher their sales. The higher their sales the more they could spend on advertising. Small brands couldn't complete.

This is how brand building worked before the internet.

Search Costs & Brands Post Internet

Now when we want to know if a brand or item is trustworthy we turn to online reviews. Online reviews lower our search costs further while increasing our decision confidence.

Online reviews also save us more money. We buy cheaper unknown generic brands because online reviews provide the social proof we need.

The virtuous advertising cycle is over too.

Small brands don't need to pay for a large national print and TV advertising campaign. They can build their band cheaply through digital marketing. La Croix seltzer water built its brand on Instagram.

Dollar Shave Club, a competitor to P&G's Gillette shave brand and now a part of Unilever, made its name with viral videos.

Because of these shifts, Procter & Gamble has lost market share in key categories. Dollar Shave Club and Harry's are both online razor subscription services. Both companies have taken market share away from Gillette.

Razor Wars

Long dominant, Gillette has seen sales of its men's razors decline in the face of competition from online startups that charge less.

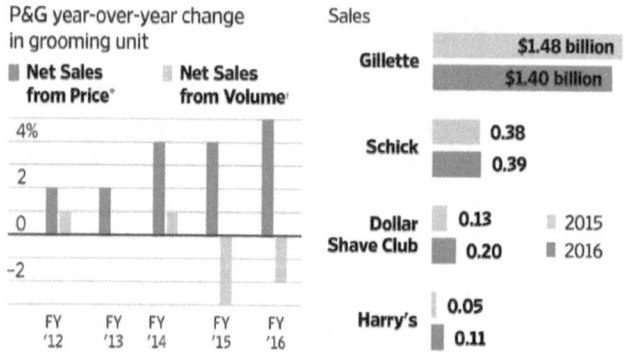

*Percentage of sales gains for the fiscal year attributable to changes in pricing and volume.
'Excluding acquisitions and divestitures   Note: Fiscal year 2016 ended June 30, 2016

Source: Euromonitor; P&G   THE WALL STREET JOURNAL.

Price increases were how P&G maintained sales growth.

Procter & Gamble cut prices across the majority of its brands because the market share loss has been too great.

Stalling organic growth has led to stalled dividend growth.

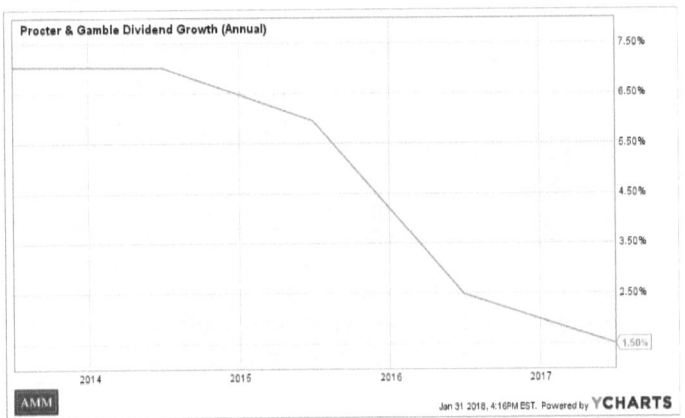

We had hoped the activist investor Nelson Peltz would push the company into breaking itself up through spin-offs. But the recent proxy fight between the two sides makes us believe this won't happen anytime soon.

We're selling Procter & Gamble now because we found a company that will split itself up into three new companies. We'll talk more about this company in an upcoming Dividend Letter.

As always, please call or email us if you have any questions about your account or if you want to discuss your portfolio strategy in greater detail.

Sincerely, .

Your Portfolio Management Team

Issue 28: Pfizer (PFE)

April 2016

Are You a Better Investor Than a Pigeon?

This is the competition. It's you versus a pigeon. Both you and the pigeon have two lights in front of you, one red and one green. You have to guess which light, red or green, will flash next. Do you think you can beat the pigeon at this game?

You're probably thinking, "Of course, I have this big beautiful brain that has put mankind on the moon. I can do better than a bird with a brain a fraction of the size of mine. Don't we call dumb people 'bird brains' for a reason?"

What if I told you the flashing lights will be completely random. Do you still think you could beat the Pigeon?

Don't worry this game has already been done as an experiment. In the experiment, people were measured against both rats and pigeons. Each subject received a reward after guessing correctly which light flashed next. The flashing lights were completely random but the green light flashed over 80% of the time. The optimal strategy is guessing green every time. You'll be right 80% of the time.

The rats and pigeons figured out this strategy fairly quickly. The human subjects figured it out quickly too. So it was a tie, right? Wrong.

After a little bit of trial and error, **the rats and pigeons guessed green every time and scored an 80% success rate. The people on average scored a 69% accuracy**. Why? Because of that big beautiful brain of yours.

Humans are the smartest species and we know it. Because we are so smart, we are overconfident in our ability to predict future events. Maybe the green light flashed several times in a row and the human subjects just "knew" that the red light would flash next. Even though they were told that the flashes would be completely random. On average the human subjects guessed red 1 out of 5 times and this dropped their accuracy to 69%.

The pigeon and the rat do not suffer the same illusions. They just know that if they guess green every time they have a very good chance of getting a reward.

We can't help ourselves. As humans, **we look for patterns and causal relationships in everything**. A section in the left hemisphere of our brain drives this. It leads us to believe with just the right amount of data we can figure out the pattern and predict what is going to happen next.

Our desire to find patterns combined with our overconfidence gets us into trouble with complex data like investing.

Investors, professional and amateur, spend a lot of time looking at charts trying to figure out the next wiggle of the stock market. They then trade in and out of the market based on what they think will happen next. What usually happens is they are wrong and they've guaranteed themselves a loss of money through excessive trading fees.

Take the beginning of this year, 2016, for example. The stock market had its worst start since at least 1897.

 **Howard Silverblatt**
@hsilverb

 Follow

At 10:30 a.m., $DJIA YTD 10.03% decline is the worst ever (1897), with the $SPX off 10.05% second to the 2009 10.85% opening 12-day decline

RETWEETS LIKES
11   10

7:39 AM - 20 Jan 2016

Based on past charts and historical patterns it was all but a certainty that the stock market would continue to go down. Nothing was more extreme than the Royal Bank of Scotland's announcement to "sell everything" and that "2016 will be a cataclysmic year".

What happened if you listened to RBS on January 12, 2016 and sold everything?

The S&P 500 is up over 6%. Even after the worse start to any year since 1897 the S&P 500 is flat for 2016. To be fair, we're only a few months into 2016.

By trying to guess when the stock market will decline next, what RBS and others are doing is guessing when the red light will flash next. We know the red light will eventually flash. We know the stock market will eventually go down but we do not know when. The day-to-day, month-to-month, even year-to-year price fluctuations of the equity market are random. **The stock market is a dynamic system with hundreds of interacting variables and overlapping feedback loops. Guessing future moves with near certainty is impossible**.

Here's the good news. Just like in the flashing light experiment above we don't need to guess the short-term moves of the stock market. We have data on the equity markets that is equivalent to the green light flashing 80% of the time.

The following table is from A Wealth of Common Sense. It shows the percentage chance of having a positive total return given a specific time period.

S&P 500: 1926-2015

Time Frame	Positive	Negative
Daily	54%	46%
Quarterly	68%	32%
One Year	74%	26%
5 Years	86%	14%
10 Years	94%	6%
20 Years	100%	0%

Source: Returns 2.0

The longer we stay invested the better our odds of having positive total returns. According to Ben Carlson, The worst 20 year period for total returns was 54% and the worst 30 year period was 854%.

The objective of investing is the same as the simple light flashing experiment, to maximize our rewards. Trying to guess what equity markets will do tomorrow, next week, or next month and then trading in and out of the stock market to try and catch these moves will only harm our portfolios and ruin our potential to maximize our long-term investing rewards.

We need to focus on what we can control. Finding quality companies and paying a fair price for them.

Sincerely,

Your Portfolio Management Team

Dividend Stock in Focus

Pfizer, Inc. (PFE): $32.76

Price as of the close April 7, 2016

Pfizer is the world's largest pharmaceutical company based on global sales. But everyone knows it for that little blue pill. You know the one that seems to have a lot of TV ads during golf tournaments for some reason.

We first bought Pfizer in our dividend growth portfolio in September of 2011 because we thought they were extremely cheap and because Pfizer is a dividend stalwart, a company that raises its dividend year-in and year-out.

We've continued to add to Pfizer because its intrinsic value has increased over the years and because CEO Ian Read is on a path of restructuring. Mr. Read is streamlining operations by spinning off non-core divisions like Zoetis (ZTS) and acquiring acquisitions for its core businesses like generic drug maker Hospira.

Mr. Read might potentially split Pfizer up even further in order to pursue his ultimate goal of lowering Pfizer's tax bill by moving out of the U.S.

Dividend History

Following its purchase of Wyeth, Inc. for $68 billion in 2009, Pfizer cut its dividend so that it could quickly repay the debt issued for the buyout. After cutting its dividend down to a quarterly rate of $0.16 per share, Pfizer now pays $0.30 per share on a quarterly basis. Since February 2009, Pfizer has grown its dividend at a compound annual rate of 9.5%.

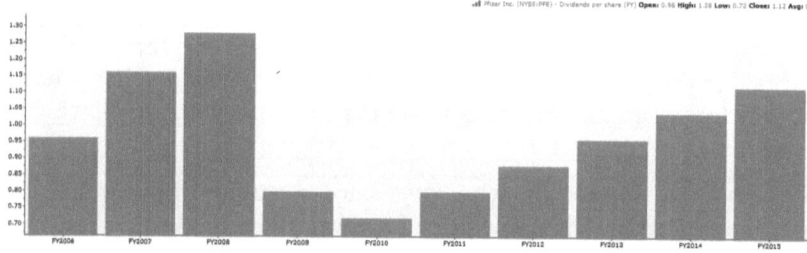

From S&P Capital IQ

Catalysts for Dividend Growth & Capital Appreciation

~~Allergan Merger~~

Pfizer and Allergan agreed to a $160 billion merger. The deal was structured as a tax inversion. By merging with Allergan, Pfizer would move its country of domicile from the U.S. to Ireland. Ireland's corporate tax rate is 12.5% versus the 35% U.S. corporate tax rate. The U.S. also taxes U.S. corporations on any profit made overseas that is brought back, "repatriated", to the U.S. If Pfizer redomiciles in Ireland through a merger with Allergan, Pfizer can reinvest those profits back into its U.S. operations without incurring a tax because it is no longer a U.S. company. Pfizer currently has over $50 billion in cash overseas.

The tax savings alone make a deal like this very attractive but the combined potential of the two companies was even more attractive.

Unfortunately, the deal is no more.

As we were writing this, the Treasury Department released a set of new aggressive anti-tax inversion laws. The new laws specifically target the Pfizer and Allergan merger and because of the new laws Pfizer and Allergan have scrapped the merger.

Pfizer's CEO Ian Read is set on moving Pfizer out of the U.S. to bring the company's costs in line with its non-U.S. based competitors. While it won't be through a merger with Allergan, Mr. Read will likely find a way to redomicile Pfizer out of the U.S. It may take splitting Pfizer up into 3 separate businesses to do so.

Spin-Offs?

Before the Allergan deal was announced, Pfizer told shareholders that at the end of 2016 management would announce whether it was going to split the company up through a series of spin-offs. Expectations for at least one spin-off grew when Pfizer bought Hospira in a bid to boost the value of Pfizer's generic and biosimilar business. Then the Allergan deal took priority and Pfizer's management postponed the split up decision until the end of 2018.

Now that the Allergan deal has been canceled. Pfizer is free to continue its spin-off plans unless another merger candidate appears.

The SEC requires 3 years of financial reports broken out by division before a business unit can be spun-off. Pfizer started reporting on its 3 business divisions in 2014. The minimum expectation is for Pfizer to separate its Established Business (generic drugs and drugs soon to be off patent) from its Innovative drug business (recently approved drugs and drugs still in development).

A brief sum of the parts analysis for Pfizer's three business divisions using Earnings Before Interest and Taxes (EBIT) values Pfizer at $43 per share.

$ in billions			
Division	EBIT TTM	Multiple	Value
Global Innovative Pharmaceutical	$7,757.00	12	$93,084.00
Global Vaccines, Oncology & Consumer Health	$6,507.00	14	$91,098.00
Global Established Pharmaceutical	$12,885.00	9	$115,965.00
Total Value			**$300,147.00**
Less Debt			($28,952.00)
Equity Value			$271,195.00
Total Shares Outstanding			6,184.10
Per Share Value			**$43.85**

Promising Pipeline & Ibrance

Over the last few years, Pfizer's revenue has declined due in part to a couple of key drugs losing patent protection. Pfizer lost the patent on Lipitor, on of the most commercially successful drugs ever, in late 2011. The company has been working hard to come up with new drugs to replace the lost revenue. That effort is starting to pay off with some 90 potential new drugs in the pipeline. One of Pfizer's most promising new drugs is Ibrance.

Ibrance is a specific breast cancer treatment and it is in stage 3/registration phase with the FDA. Estimates of peak sales are $10-15 Billion with Ibrance potentially reaching $4 billion in annual sales by 2020. Ibrance targets metastatic breast cancer and in combination with AstraZeneca's Faslodex (an estrogen blocker) patients survived on average 9.2 months before their cancer worsened. The control group survived 3.8 months.

Pfizer is working on more indications for Ibrance which could push annual sales well past the estimated $4-5 billion annual sales.

Biotech Buyout

Pfizer could get bigger through a buyout or merger first, before they pursue spinoffs. They have the balance sheet to buy another biotech company in an effort to increase their roster of promising new drugs. Shares in biotech companies are still trading well below their peak last year and the cheaper prices may entice Pfizer to pursue one more buyout before separating the company.

Pre-Mortem (Potential Risks to our Thesis)

More Anti-Inversion Laws

As we were writing this the Treasury Department released a set of new aggressive laws aimed to stop Tax Inversion deals. The wording of the new laws suggests that the authors were targeting the Pfizer and Allergan deal. There are some big questions with these new laws including why is the Treasury Department, part of the Executive Branch, and not Congress writing these new laws? And why are the laws being changed and applied on an ex-post facto basis? The new laws also seem to change the meaning of what constitutes a share, or ownership in a company.

Pfizer is looking for a way to move out of the U.S. The company has now had two deals scuttled because of changing tax laws. Staying in the U.S. does not mean Pfizer will go out of business, however, it does mean Pfizer will have less capital to reinvest into its business versus its foreign-based peers. For an industry built on R&D, every bit of capital reinvestment helps. Over time as Pfizer's foreign peers reinvest more into their businesses they will slowly out compete Pfizer.

Pipeline Wipeout

Pfizer's pipeline of new drugs, especially its breast cancer drug, is very attractive. However, we don't know with certainty what the future will bring. Pfizer's potential blockbusters may not be blockbusters and the revenue Pfizer has lost from Lipitor may not be regained. For sustained dividend growth, we need business growth.

Conclusion

With the Allergan deal no longer an option, our base case estimate of fair value for Pfizer using a discounted cash flow model is $40 per share. A sum of the parts estimate of Pfizer's fair value is around $43 per share. If Pfizer's pipeline, especially Ibrance, turns out to be as successful as currently estimated then Pfizer is worth more.

Pfizer's share price had been under pressure as arbitrage funds sold Pfizer shares short and went long Allergan shares in anticipation of the deal closing. Now that the deal is off Pfizer's share price has popped as the arbitrage funds unwind their positions. Pfizer may give back some of its gains from the last few days as the buying pressure subsides, but in the long run we expect the company to offer favorable returns from current levels.

Issue 29: Pepsi (PEP)

June 2016

Plane Crashes, Stock Market Crashes, & Why We Overestimate Them

For the sake of argument let's say you're afraid of flying, but you have a wedding to go to on the other side of the country and you'll have to fly to get there. Right before you get on that plane I ask you, "What are the odds of your plane crashing?"

I agree, this is a terrible question to ask someone who is afraid of flying right before they get on a plane. However, the emotional element is necessary as we'll see later on. So how likely, expressed as a percentage, is your plane to crash? 1, 2, 5, 10%?

Since you're afraid of flying you find yourself recalling with great ease several recent airplane crashes. The missing Malaysian plane, the Germanwings crash in the Alps, the Korean Air runway crash in San Francisco, etc. You also realize crashes don't happen all the time but they do come up fairly often on the news. So you argue yourself into a 1% chance of your plane crashing.

At 1% you would be overestimating your odds of a crash by an extreme amount. Your chances to be in any commercial aviation mishap is 1 in 11 million. If you want the odds for your specific flight in your specific plane there's an app for that.

Am I going down?

LHR ✈ JFK

Virgin Atlantic
Airbus A330

1 in 5,371,369

You'd expect to go down if you
took this flight every day for

14,716 years

Rate   Share   Apps

Let's do another thought experiment. Similar to the emotions an airplane crash invokes.

Stock Market Crashes

How likely will the stock market crash in the next 6 months? We'll define a crash as a one-day decline greater than 12%.

Just like the airplane crashes above you easily recall the 2008 financial crisis, the 2000 tech bubble bursting, Black Monday in 1987, the Flash Crash. Even the beginning of this year started off with a 12% decline. What is your guess at the chance of an equity market crash within the next 6 months? 5, 10, 20%.

If you're like most people you probably guessed close to 20%.

The National Bureau of Economic Research sends out a survey asking investors this exact same question. They've been doing this for 26 years and **on average the respondents put the chances of a market crash over the next 6 months at 19%.**

Just like overestimating airplane crashes the average investor is overestimating the odds of a market crash. From Mark Hulbert's piece in Barron's Stop Worrying About the Stock Market Crashing.

> Xavier Gabaix, a finance professor at New York University, has derived a crash-frequency formula that he believes captures a

universal trait of all markets, not just equity markets or those in the U.S. According to that formula, **the odds of a 12.8% crash in any given six-month period are 0.92%**, almost as low as the actual frequency in the U.S. stock market over the last century.

Why do we drastically overestimate the odds of plane crashes, stock market crashes, and other catastrophes?

Availability Heuristic

The Availability Heuristic is another important quirk in our thinking processes. When we asked you about the chances of a plane crash or a stock market crash did you compile all of the relevant data to mathematically derive your answer? Probably not. That is a lot of work.

What your brain did was substitute the hard question with an easier one, **"How easily can I recall past events?"**

You could easily recall recent plane crashes and stock crashes and these became the most relevant data to answer the question.

The more salient the event the more attention you pay to it and the more easily that event is recalled from memory. Plane crashes and stock market crashes are extremely salient events receiving national multi-day coverage. When asked about them you easily recall past disasters and then overestimate their likelihood in the future. What you do not recall are all the non-events. All the flights that made it to their destination safely or all the days, weeks and months when stock markets are calm.

The more recent an event has occurred the more were likely to overestimate its chances too. When stock markets have experienced a period of losses right before the National Bureau of Economic Research survey has been sent out, respondents increased their odds of a market crash. The same effect happens when the news and other media talk more about market losses or use the word crash.

Stock Crashes - A Red Herring Risk?

Perhaps most damaging is the red-herring effect that the availability heuristic often provides. Investors focused on the small but dramatic risks of a market crash, often miss the more nuanced risks being realized right in front of them. Take the investor worried about a market crash; he chooses to shift to the safety of cash until "things calm down". His cash earns nearly zero so immediately inflation begins eating away at his purchasing power. This is a risk with a near 100% certainty of happening.

Even worse, however, is that by going to cash he has eliminated from his portfolio the opportunity for upside. If the great crash doesn't come to fruition he must make a decision: buy back in at higher prices or continue to wait for the crash while his cash savings are eroded by inflation. Neither is a good decision and both are wealth destructive. In one case inflation continues to slowly eat away at his wealth, in the other he sold low and bought high.

Of course, a third option is that he is right about the pending crash and times his exit near the top. Now he has a second decision, when to re-enter? If he is like most investors, he will wait until markets are calm again (i.e. at higher prices) so while he avoided much of the downside it was ultimately for nothing. Additionally, if he sold dividend paying investments when he went to cash then he missed out on the additional cash flow these investments provide.

It is for this reason that **of our firm's five core principals we rank Asset Allocation number one**. If you can't sleep at night because of your portfolio's volatility, it may mean you have too much invested in stocks and should re-evaluate your portfolio strategy to include more conservative non-stock assets. Alternatively, it could mean that your asset allocation is just fine but you're being held hostage by the availability heuristic. In either case, tune out the financial media (which tends to exaggerate market events to attract viewers) and call us to determine if any changes to your strategy are in order.

We can never fully remove our biases or gain control over our irrational thinking processes. What we can do is be aware of them. When we have to make important decisions, **it is important to slow down and review our decision-making process**. We need to ask ourselves if we're making a rational decision or one based on emotions.

Stock markets will decline. It is a normal part of a functioning market, and a critical part of the risk-reward dynamic in investing. There can be no reward without risk. Another of our core investment principles is "the price you pay determines your return", so market declines should be viewed through the lens of opportunity since they allow investors the opportunity to buy lower thus increasing their long-term return potential.

Sincerely,

Your Portfolio Management Team

Dividend Stock in Focus

Pepsi Co. (PEP): $102.84

Price as of the close June 9, 2016

When you hear Pepsi you probably think soda. A soda originally called Brad's Drink which was a mixture of pepsin (a digestive enzyme), kola nut, vanilla, and sugar.

But Pepsi is now so much more than Soda. Today, Pepsi owns 22 well-known brands that each generate over $1 billion in revenue

Pepsi owns a lot other brands outside of soda too, including Sabra Hummus, Naked Juices, and Stacy Pita Chips.

Not bad for a company that went bankrupt twice during the early 20th century and was almost bought by Coca-Cola three times during the 1920s and 1930s.

Dividend History

Over the last 10 years, Pepsi has grown their annual dividend at a compound annual rate of 9.05%. Pepsi has been paying and growing its dividend for 43 years. The foundation for your dividend growth portfolio is dividend stalwarts. Companies like Pepsi with well known and loved brands that stand the test of time. This allows a company like Pepsi to maintain pricing power and grow their dividend year-in and year-out.

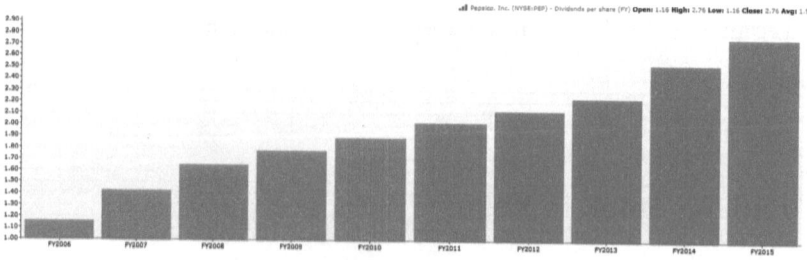

From S&P Capital IQ

Catalysts for Dividend Growth & Capital Appreciation

Frito Lay

Pepsi's future is more about food than soda. The crown jewel of Pepsi's food business is its Frito-Lay division. Frito-Lay generates 23% of Pepsi's revenue but it contributes over 39% to Pepsi's operating profit.

The snack business is growing while Pepsi's carbonated drink business is under pressure. More on this in the Pre-Mortem below. In North America, Frito-Lay commands a 25% market share while none of its competitors have a market share higher than single digits. Frito-lay also sports industry leading operating margins.

Operational Efficiency

A couple years ago Pepsi attracted a large activist investor in Trian Partners, run by Nelson Peltz. One of Trian's main points was that Pepsi's food business was subsidizing Pepsi's beverage business. The food business was growing with large operating margins. The beverage business, mainly soda, was shrinking and had lower margins than food. The other point was that each business, both food and beverage, had its own corporate structure and then there was the added layer of the overarching parent corporation's operating structure. Pepsi's corporate structure was too bloated. The food and beverage businesses we're not operating in tandem to reduce overall corporate costs.

The presence of the activist investor motivated Pepsi's top management to push for greater synergies between its two businesses and to reduce costs at every level. Pepsi is currently about $5 billion into a $9 billion cost savings plan. Better operational efficiency means less capital is needed to reinvest back into the business to help it grow. This leaves more cash for Pepsi to buy back shares and increase its dividend.

Pepsi already generated high returns on capital and equity but after the recent initiative by management, returns have crept upwards as margins have improved too.

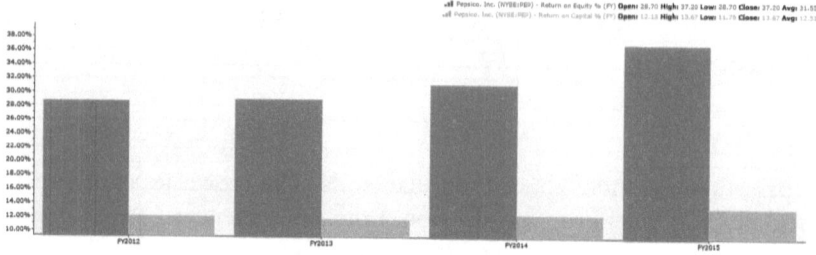

Data from S&P Capital IQ

Spin-Off?

We first started buying Pepsi for clients in January 2012. At the time, Pepsi was cheap on an absolute basis and extremely cheap when compared to other companies with similar portfolios of valuable brands. Pepsi's low price combined with such valuable brands made it an attractive target for activist investors.

Trian Partners took a large stake in Pepsi and then authored a white paper on why the company should be split into two, a drink business and a snack business. Pepsi pushed back on the break-up but worked with Trian Partners in achieving cost savings and improving operations. Trian's activism ended last month, May 2016, when they sold their shares in Pepsi after a couple years of very good gains.

Even though Trian Partners is out and no immediate catalyst exists for splitting up Pepsi, the possibility still exists. As we'll discuss below in the Pre-Mortem, soda consumption habits are changing and if carbonated drinks become too much of a drag on the true value of Pepsi's snack business then the two companies should be split up.

Or Merger?

The other possibility is Frito-Lay buying another food company like Mondelez (MDLZ). It would be a combination of Mondelez' portfolio of sweets with Frito-Lay's portfolio of salty food.

Mondelez is the international business of the former Kraft. Mondelez formed when Kraft split itself into two businesses. At one time post spin-off, Mondelez was viewed as the better company to buy but it has struggled lately. Mondelez has attracted its own activist investor, Bill Ackman, and the odds are he will push for a sale of the company. The only two contenders right now to buy Mondelez are Pepsi and Kraft Heinz (KHC), another portfolio holding.

A merger of this magnitude would fundamentally change Pepsi's operations and it would most likely lead to a spin-off of the beverage business so that Frito-Lay can focus solely on its larger food business.

Nelson Peltz and Trian were big proponents of Pepsi buying Mondelez but they just sold their shares. Trian still has a person on the Pepsi board but Trian's sway in matters is greatly reduced. The other proponent for a sale of Mondelez would be Bill Ackman. Bill is currently distracted with two other large positions that are deeply hurting his fund. A short position in Herbalife (HLF) and a long position in Valeant Pharmaceuticals. Herbalife and Valeant have hurt Bill Ackman's fund so much that he has sold off some of his stake in Mondelez to help regain control of his portfolio.

The likelihood of an activist lead merger is dimming but it could still be championed by current management.

Pre-Mortem (Potential Risks to our Thesis)

Changing Consumer Drink Tastes

Soda consumption is on the decline in most developed markets. In the U.S. soda consumption has been declining for the last 11 years. Lead by diet sodas.

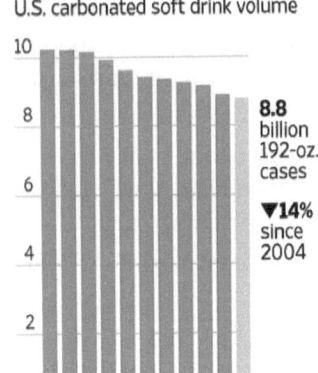

Soda Slump

U.S. carbonated soft drink volume

8.8 billion 192-oz. cases

▼**14%** since 2004

Source: Beverage Digest

THE WALL STREET JOURNAL.

Chart courtesy of The Wall Street Journal.

Snacks are the crown jewel of Pepsi right now but beverage sales are a large generator of free cash flow for Pepsi. This free cash fuels dividend growth and share buybacks. Decreased demand will affect Pepsi's overall growth and the growth of its dividend. Soda is essentially the new cigarette. Can Pepsi and other soda companies raise prices to offset volume decline like the tobacco companies do? Can Pepsi and other soda companies reduce costs and improve efficiencies like tobacco companies to keep growing free cash flow?

Like cigarettes, soda is now facing demands for taxes to reduce its consumption.

Sugar Tax

Excessive sugar intake is considered to be one of the reasons we are seeing higher rates of obesity and diabetes. It is not the only reason. Like a lot of health issues, it is a combination of factors but that doesn't stop policy makers and activists from singling out one item as the root cause. In a gross oversimplification of a larger problem, sugary drinks, most notably soda, have been labeled as the main culprit for higher obesity rates.

The solution put forth is to tax soda in the hope that higher costs will lower consumption. Higher tax rates have helped lower smoking rates in the U.S. Recent reports out of Mexico show a decline in soda consumption after the implementation of their soda tax. It is still too early to tell if this is causation or just correlation. The main goal is lower obesity rates. Reduction of calories from one food source is usually replaced by another. If that new food source is full of added sugar than nothing changes. Likewise, no study has yet shown a decline in obesity rates after an introduction of a soda tax.

The absence of clear factual data has never stopped public policy makers from making large decisions before. There is a good chance we will see more and more soda taxes. The higher cost of soda will likely effect Pepsi's carbonated drink business for the worse.

Conclusion

When we first bought Pepsi we believed the company was undervalued. The discrepancy between price and value did not last long, especially when Trian Partners got involved. Since then Pepsi has traded at or slightly above our estimate of fair value which has made it tough to continue to add to our position. We currently value Pepsi at $105 per share. Even the news of Trian Partners selling their stake in Pepsi hasn't taken its share price down far enough to where we would like to buy more Pepsi. Newer accounts may not have exposure to Pepsi, yet. As soon as Pepsi trades at a big enough discount to our estimate of fair value we expect to add to the position.

Issue 30: Wells Fargo (WFC)

July 2016

The "F" Word and Hidden Risks

Got your attention? The F word we are talking about here is FIDUCIARY.

The Department of Labor (DOL) recently passed the Fiduciary Rule which, among other things, requires that advisors to retirement plans act as fiduciaries. A fiduciary is required by law to act in their clients best interests. This differs from a lesser standard called the Suitability Rule that most stock brokers and financial sales professionals are held to. The suitability standard requires that they recommend suitable investments, however these investments don't necessarily have to be in the clients' best interest.

This may seem like boring minutiae and legalese, but we think a Fiduciary relationship should be the cornerstone of the investment advisor – client relationship. At AMM we act as fiduciaries on all client relationships, and have since the inception of our firm. While the Fiduciary standard doesn't guarantee great performance, or even any particular level of skill, it does require the person or firm you are dealing with to put your interests first when providing investment advice. An obvious starting point, in our opinion, when hiring an investment advisor.

Hidden Risk

The Fiduciary rule reminds us too, that Risk is much more than just the probability of permanent capital loss. There are other hidden or not readily observable risks that are often overlooked by investors. Using the example above, hiring a non-fiduciary advisor likely increases your risk of being exposed to advice that is not in your best interest. While this may seem self-evident, we have rarely met with a prospective client who asked whether or not we were a fiduciary.

Another common, but hidden risk is inflation. Most of us are aware of the mathematical concept of inflation. A stamp costs 49 cents today vs. 32 cents 20 years ago – representing an increase of more than 2% per year. However when it comes to decision making people often ignore or, at a minimum, don't fully comprehend the risk of inflation.

In a recent Wall Street Journal article by Jason Zweig he referenced a classic experiment where people were asked who would be happier: someone who got a 2% yearly raise when inflation was zero or someone who got a 5% raise when inflation was 4%. While the person receiving the 2% raise would be better off in real terms, two-thirds of those surveyed said the person with the 5% raise would be happier. Evidently the "bigger raise" provided a psychological happiness benefit that trumped the real increase in wealth.

Some investors may currently be opting for a "conservative return" in bank CDs or short-term government bonds at rates well below inflation instead of investing in more volatile investments with higher return potential. For investors with short term money this is entirely reasonable, but for investors with a long time horizon they are essentially trading a negative real return for the comfort of limited volatility. As we often say, volatility is not risk. Real risk is the likelihood of permanent capital loss, and long-term investors in cash, CDs and money market are nearly guaranteeing this at current interest rate levels.

The investment landscape is riddled with these psychological minefields, and is one of the reasons we focus so heavily on investor psychology in these periodic updates. For a deeper read on the subjects of behavioral finance and investor psychology we strongly recommend "Thinking Fast & Slow" by Daniel Kahneman and "Your Money & Your Brain" by Jason Zweig.

Sincerely,

Your Portfolio Management Team

Dividend Stock in Focus

Wells Fargo (WFC): $48.30

Price as of the close July 21, 2016

For most of Civilization's history, the size of the economy was pretty much fixed. To become wealthy meant someone else became poor.

Then something changed. As Yuval Noah Harari points out in his book "Sapiens: A Brief History of Humankind"

> "In 1500 annual per capita production averaged $550, while today every man, woman and child produces, on the average, $8,800 a year."

What spurred this immense growth?

CREDIT.

While credit had existed in one form or another since the dawn of civilization, the credit offered was typically small and the rates high. If the economic pie was fixed why lend out large sums of money to bet on future growth?

During the Scientific Revolution, the idea of progress came about. If we invest our resources in research and exploration we will create better technologies and make new discoveries that will increase the sum total of human production. The economic pie can grow and wealth can be created without taking someone else's slice.

A hopeful outlook on the future allowed people and institutions to believe in and use credit as a means to fund future growth. Credit became more freely available and offered at more reasonable rates.

As much as we love to gripe about banks, they are the institutions that provide the credit to fund our economic dreams.

Wells Fargo started in 1852 to provide banking, financial services, and most importantly credit to one of America's biggest economic dreams, the westward expansion.

Dividend History

Like all the major banks, Wells Fargo had to cut its dividend during the financial crisis. The cut was necessary to maintain adequate capital reserve ratios as balance sheet write-offs and loan loss reserves increased during the tumultuous time. Since cutting its quarterly dividend down to $0.05 per share in May 2009, Wells Fargo has increased its quarterly dividend to $0.38, a 39.5% compound annual growth rate. In 2014, Wells Fargo's total annual dividends paid surpassed its pre-financial crisis high.

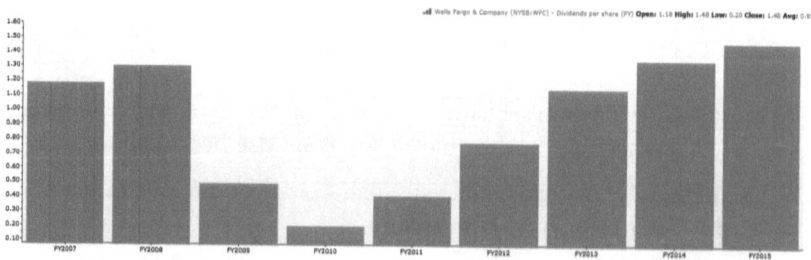

From S&P Capital IQ.

Catalysts for Dividend Growth & Capital Appreciation

Asset Growth

Wells Fargo recently bought several pieces of General Electric's (GE) loan portfolio including half of GE's commercial real estate portfolio and their entire railcar services business. The added efficiency of integrating the portfolio should add around $300 million of net interest income. Wells Fargo's efficiency ratio on the new portfolio additions should increase too, as they sell other services to its new customer base of around 160,000 relationships. While these customers had previously only had credit deals with GE, Wells Fargo now has the opportunity to expand the relationships with other commercial banking offerings.

The chart below shows Wells Fargo's wholesale business loan growth including the recent GE asset purchases.

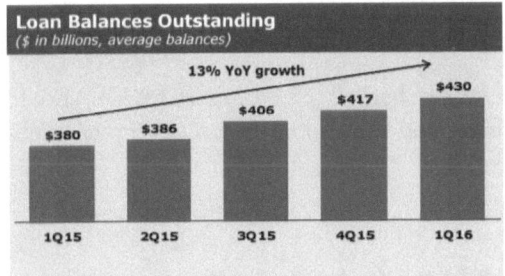

Loans

- Broad-based loan growth across businesses
- $12.6B from 2Q15 GE Capital loan purchase and financing transaction
- $0.9B loans from GE Railcar Services closed 1/1/16 ($3.2B in operating lease assets)
- $24.0B from North American portions of GE Capital acquisition recorded in balances closed on 3/1/16 ($2.7B in operating lease assets)

Chart from WFC Presentation May 24, 2016.

Higher Interest Rates

One way a bank makes money off deposits is the spread between the interest a bank pays on a savings account and the interest received from buying short-term US treasury bills. The interest paid by short-term Treasury bill is based on the Fed Funds rate which currently sits at 0.25%. The interest rate banks pay on savings accounts are equally as low and the spread between the two has tightened.

Net interest margin measures the amount of income generated by a bank's assets to the interest it pays out to its lenders including its savings accounts. The spread between interest paid on savings accounts and interest received from treasuries is one component of the net interest margin. As you can see in the chart below Wells Fargo's Net interest Margin is at its lowest level within the last 10 years.

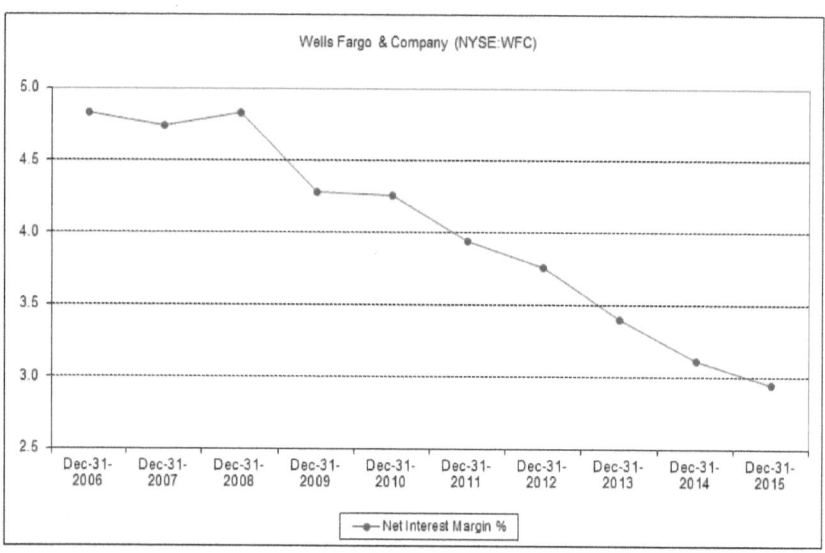

Data from S&P Capital IQ.

When or if interest rates rise, Wells Fargo's Net Interest Margin should rise too increasing its profitability and increasing the excess capital Wells Fargo can return to shareholders.

High Switching Costs

How often do you switch banks? Do you change checking accounts every time the bank across the street offers a new incentive? We're going to assume you don't. It's highly likely that you're still with the same bank where you opened up your very first account. That bank may have changed names over the years as banks consolidated but you personally didn't change where your account was held.

Even though checking and savings accounts are pretty much exactly the same at every bank, we don't switch banks when one offers a slightly better deal. Once we've set up a bank account it's a hassle to change. We have to get new checks, new debit cards, establish a new bill pay system, etc. The incentives to change banks has to be large enough to make it worth the effort. It usually isn't. Customers tend to stick with their banks for a very long time.

Product Per Customer

The more products a bank customer has with their bank - savings account, checking account, credit card, mortgage, car loan - the higher the switching costs become, and the more profitable that relationship is for the bank. This is true for both retail customers and corporate customers.

The efficiency ratio (Non-Interest Expenses/Revenue) is a way to measure this profitability. It is far less costly to generate more revenue per existing customer than to gain new customers. The efficiency ratio is also a good proxy for how well a bank controls costs in general. The lower the number the better.

The chart below compares Wells Fargo's efficiency ratio (dark blue line) to the other big banks: Bank of America (BAC), JP Morgan Chase (JPM), Citigroup (C).

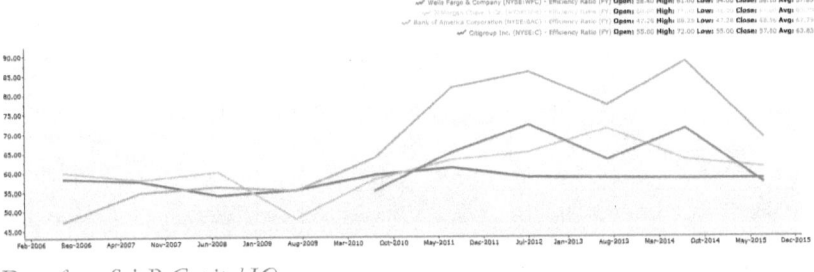

Data from S&P Capital IQ.

Pre-Mortem (Potential Risks to our Thesis)

Continued Low or Negative Interest Rates

The current low-interest rate policy by the Federal Reserve is hurting Wells Fargo's profitability. After Janet Yellen raised the Fed Funds Rate up to 0.25% from zero in December of 2015, the expectation for more rate increases rose as well. The Federal Reserve had the opportunity to raise rates a few times since then but didn't.

Now with the fallout of Britain potentially leaving the EU (the referendum is non-binding) hanging over financial markets, the Fed appears unlikely to raise rates anytime soon. Right now markets are expecting that the Federal Reserve won't raise rates for at least another year.

99 Export Data   World Interest Rate Probability
United States   ▾   Instrument Futures: Fed Funds   ▾   FED Effective Rate 0.39
1) Overview   2) Future Implied Probability
Current Implied Probabilities   3) Add/Remove Rate
Dates   ⊙ Meeting   ● Calculation   Calculated 06/24/2016 ▦ Based on rate 0.25-0.50

Meeting	Prob Of Hike	Prob of Cut	0-0.25	0.25-0.5	0.5-0.75
07/27/2016	0.0%	8.0%	8.0%	92.0%	0.0%
09/21/2016	0.0%	8.0%	8.0%	92.0%	0.0%
11/02/2016	0.0%	8.0%	8.0%	92.0%	0.0%
12/14/2016	12.9%	6.9%	6.9%	80.2%	12.9%
02/01/2017	12.9%	6.9%	6.9%	80.2%	12.9%

Historical Analysis for Meeting 07/27/2016 ▾   4) Add/Remove Serie

■ 0-0.25   8.00
■ 0.25-0.5 92.00
■ 0.5-0.75 0.00

Mar   Jun   Sep   Dec   Mar   Jun
        2015   2016
                          Historical Date

Australia 61 2 9777 8600 Brazil 5511 2395 9000 Europe 44 20 7330 7500 Germany 49 69 9204 1210 Hong Kong 852 2977 6000
Japan 81 3 3201 8900   Singapore 65 6212 1000   U.S. 1 212 318 2000   Copyright 2016 Bloomberg Finance L.P.
                                          SN 182055 H444-939-2 24-Jun-16 10:33:34 EDT GMT-4:00

Odds of a Rate Hike from Bloomberg.

A continued low-interest rate environment means a continued low net interest margin for Wells Fargo. A lower for longer net interest margin means less capital to return to shareholders through dividends and share buybacks.

Regulation

After the 2008 financial crisis and passage of the Dodd-Frank Act, systemically important banks are now required to submit a capital return plan to the Federal Reserve for review. If the Federal Reserve doesn't think the bank is adequately capitalized or well reserved it can cancel the banks' capital return plan. Essentially all dividend increases and share buybacks must be approved by a third party. It is no longer up to the discretion of the bank.

Wells Fargo is extremely well reserved and capitalized but that doesn't mean the Federal Reserve will always think so. Future dividend growth may be hampered by the Federal Reserve's review. A declined capital return plan doesn't mean Wells Fargo cannot pay a dividend or raise it again in the future. It means the bank will have to submit a revised plan and wait for its approval. It's possible the new plan will not include a dividend raise. This is a short-term setback because Wells Fargo has to submit its capital plan every year. Missing a dividend raise one year can be "caught-up" in the next review.

Higher Capital Ratio Requirements

Banks create value for their owners by making loans against deposits. All banks, regardless of regulations, should hold some equity reserves to protect against potential losses. The more equity reserves a bank has, the lower their returns on equity, all else being equal. The new higher equity reserve ratios required by the Dodd-Frank Act reduce the overall returns on equity that a bank can deliver.

Wells Fargo's current Return on Equity is 13.6% which is much lower than during previous economic expansionary periods. Low interest rates and a shrinking Net interest Margin play a part in lower returns on equity too.

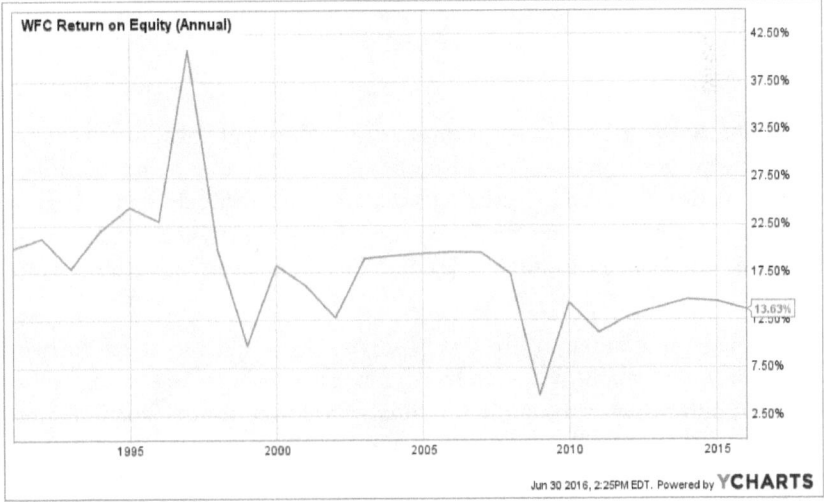

Data from YCharts.

If the regulators want the systemically significant banks to hold even more equity reserves then the returns Wells Fargo can generate will be lowered further.

Cross Selling Tapped Out

For such a large bank Wells Fargo's operations and services are pretty basic. It isn't involved with capital market activities like JP Morgan, Bank of America, or Citigroup. Wells Fargo remains consumer centric. To help reach its level of profitability while staying focused on consumers means

Wells Fargo has to sell a lot of extra services and products via cross-selling.

Cross-selling has been a core strategy at Wells Fargo for years. In 2006 their motto for products per customer was, "We're Over Five! Shooting for Six! Going for Gr-eight!". In 2016 the average number of products a Wells Fargo customer has is 6.29, however this is down from 6.36 in 2013. While a small decline, if this trend continues or accelerates it will hurt Wells Fargo's growth and future profitability.

Another issue is that by focusing so hard on cross-selling and incentivizing your employees to sell more you end up with employees engaging in aggressive and borderline illegal activities. The city of Los Angeles filed a civil lawsuit against Wells Fargo last year accusing the company of engaging in "unfair, unlawful, and fraudulent conduct through a pervasive culture of high-pressure sales". The lawsuit has now attracted the attention of Federal regulators.

Conclusion

Being the source of credit for economic growth puts banks in a favorable operating position in any capitalistic based economy. A well run bank, a bank that doesn't take big credit risks and can effectively control costs, can exist for a very long time because their product will always be in demand. The Banca Monte dei Paschi di Siena has been in existence since 1492.

Wells Fargo is comparatively young at 164 years old but it has proven itself as an extremely well-run bank. During its short 164 years, it has survived and grown through many tough economic times. Odds are very good too that it will survive the current low-interest rate, increased regulatory environment currently weighing on its stock price. Even if low-interest rates last for a longer time, as currently expected, there is still tremendous value in Wells Fargo and its banking franchise.

Using 2% per year asset growth, return on assets of 1.3%, share reduction of 1% per year, and a P/E ratio of 11, we value Wells Fargo at $60 per share. We think Wells Fargo is potentially worth a lot more if/when interest rates increase.

Issue 31: Morgan Stanley (MS)

November 2016

Pokémon Go and the Substitution Effect

If you didn't hear, Pokémon Go was a huge hit this past summer. Pokémon GO is an augmented reality smart-phone based game that integrates the classic Pokémon video and card game into the world around you.

Pokémon Go was released on July 6, 2016 and it was an overnight sensation. So many people started playing the game that the servers supporting it kept crashing. This was a worldwide phenomenon with servers crashing in every country where Pokémon Go had launched.

Based on the popularity of the game, Nintendo's share price more than doubled by July 18.

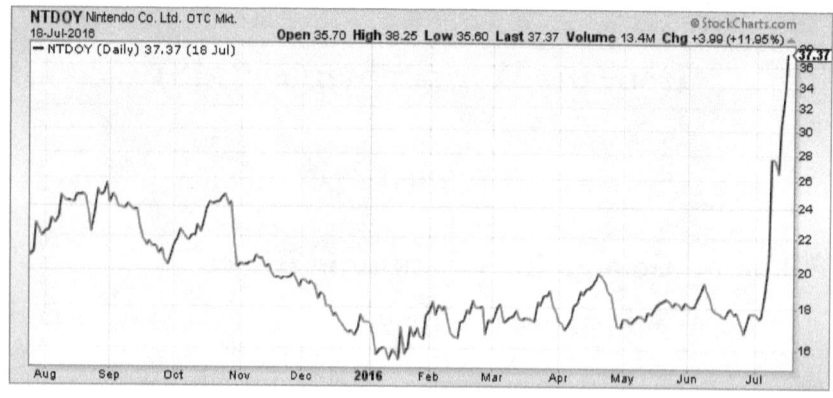

Chart courtesy of Stockcharts.com.

And rightfully so, as such a popular product means Nintendo is a great investment.

Right?

Substitution Heuristic

The substitution Heuristic happens when we are faced with a hard question. If the question is too hard or requires too much effort to figure out we subconsciously swap the hard question with an easier question.

The hard question in the above scenario is: What will be Nintendo's actual share in the profit of Pokémon Go?

Pokémon is owned by The Pokémon Company, a privately held company. Nintendo owns a third of The Pokémon Company. The game Pokémon Go was created by another privately held company Niantic. Nintendo owns a piece of Niantic too along with Google. Like all apps and games offered on iPhones and Android phones, Google and Apple get a cut of all revenue generated through in-app purchases.

Nintendo only receives a fraction of the revenue and profits Pokémon Go generates. Figuring out that share is hard but it's not impossible. It just takes time and effort.

The Easier Question

Why Nintendo's shares doubled is because investors substituted the hard question, "how much will Nintendo actually earn", with the much easier question, "is Pokémon associated with Nintendo?"

When it comes to investing, substituting the hard question with an easier question causes problems. Nintendo's ADR share price dropped more than 10% the day after Nintendo answered the hard question for everyone.

> On Friday, Nintendo sent out a warning to stockholders explaining all this: "Because of this accounting scheme, the income reflected on the Company's consolidated business results is limited." Skittish investors started to sell immediately.

Substituting an easy question for a hard one happens all the time. People buy Starbucks' stock because they drink the coffee, people buy Apple because they own its phone. What they don't do is determine the value of a company based on its current and expected cash flows and then determine a fair price to pay for the company. It's tedious work to figure this out. It is far easier to determine whether you like a product or not.

The substitution effect doesn't just happen with investing. Every hard decision we make is subject to the Substitution Effect and we can't eliminate it. It is a quirk in the way we think. When we believe we've made a completely rational decision we have in fact made a completely irrational decision.

The only checks we can place on the substitution effect is to slow down and review our decision making process. Have we really weighed all the pertinent factors? We can also enlist the help of a devil's advocate, someone to challenge our rationale.

At American Money Management we do one other thing to counteract the substitution effect. We like to write about our investment decisions. If we can't articulate our investment choices in a clear easy-to-understand way then we haven't done our research. We haven't asked the hard questions.

This issue we discuss Morgan Stanley, a semi-controversial "wall street" stock – and competitor of AMM. While we think our client offering is superior to the Morgan Stanley broker model, the stock still looks attractive on a number of levels.

Sincerely,

Your Portfolio Management Team

Dividend Stock in Focus

Morgan Stanley (MS): $38.49

Price as of the close November 11, 2016

We invest in in three types of dividend paying stocks for your portfolio.

1) Dividend Stalwarts: Companies that have strong dependable market positions, that pay a reasonable dividend (~2-3%), and have shown an ability to grow their dividends over a long period of time at a pace far faster than inflation. While the current yield is modest, we expect the growth in the dividend payout to provide a more robust yield (on original cost) in the future.

2) Restructuring/Special Situations: Companies undergoing a restructuring, spin-off, or other special situation. If we see value in the restructuring and the parent company pays a reasonable dividend we will invest. Our initial time frame for these investments is one year but if, after the restructuring, one of the companies' appears to offer good odds of becoming a dividend stalwart we may hold our investment for a longer time frame.

3) New Dividend Payers: Companies that have recently initiated a dividend policy. While these companies do not have the long history of paying and growing their dividend like the stalwarts, they do have a strong market position and the cash flow to become a stalwart in the future.

Morgan Stanley has been around since 1935. Henry S. Morgan (Grandson of J.P. Morgan) and Harold Stanley formed the company in response to the Glass-Steagall act, which required the separation of commercial and investment banking businesses after the Great Depression.

Morgan Stanley already pays a dividend and has paid one for a long time but we are classifying Morgan Stanley as a New Dividend Payer. As you'll see in the dividend history section below, Morgan Stanley cut its dividend during the financial crisis and kept it at the new lower rate until 2014. During that time Morgan Stanley has changed the focus of its core business and only recently started raising its dividend again. It is the shift in Morgan Stanley's core business that we think will allow the company to grow its dividend well into the future.

Dividend History

The chart below is not what you would expect of a dividend growth investment. A company with a massive dividend cut during the financial crisis and only two years of recent dividend growth, albeit; growth of 50% each year and an increase this quarter of 33%. This is why, even though Morgan Stanley has paid a dividend for a long time, we classify it as a "New Dividend Payer".

We see the company continuing to grow its dividend at an above-average rate over the next few years because of its changing business focus and its large capital reserves.

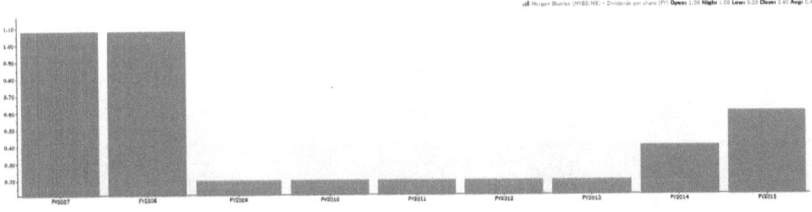

From S&P Capital IQ.

Catalysts for Dividend Growth & Capital Appreciation

Wealth Management

Before the 2008 financial crisis Morgan Stanley's profitability relied on its investment banking and trading activities. After surviving the 2008 financial crisis Morgan Stanley's management realized they could no longer rely on the erratic nature of its trading business or the cyclicality of its investment banking operations. Morgan Stanley needed a more stable revenue and profit stream and they found it in their wealth management division.

Revenue from its wealth management division has become a bigger percentage of the Morgan Stanley's total revenue.

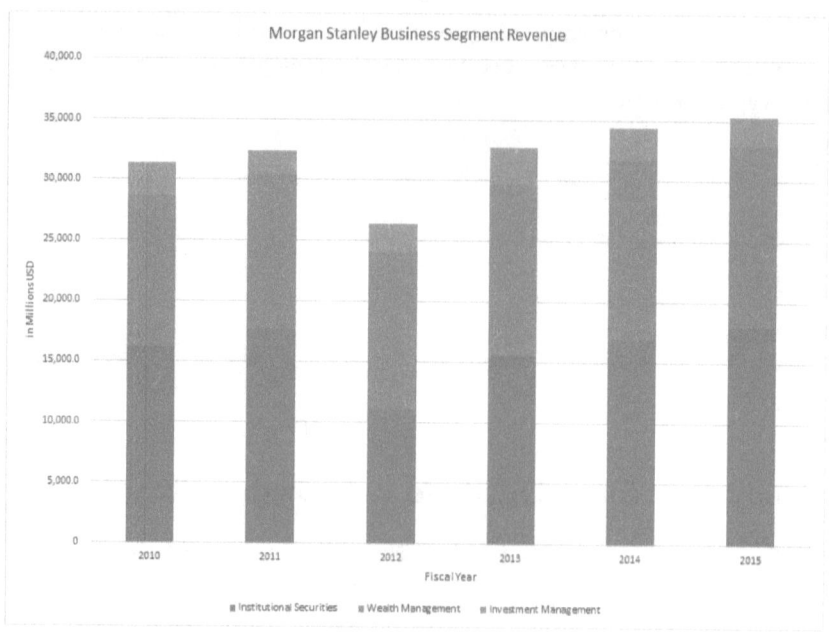

Morgan Stanley Business Segment Revenue

But it is the net profits before tax from the Wealth Management division that has provided the biggest boost to Morgan Stanley's overall profitability.

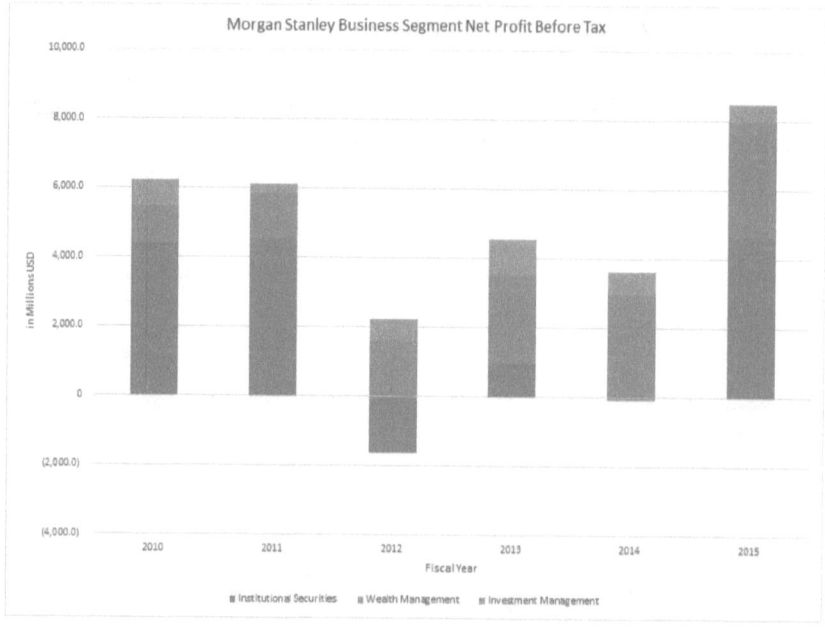

Morgan Stanley Business Segment Net Profit Before Tax

The profits from Morgan Stanley's wealth management division will still fluctuate with the overall market but they shouldn't fluctuate to the extremes that its trading and investment banking divisions do.

While Returns on equity and capital will be lower than its trading business, Morgan Stanley's wealth management should provide a more consistent and dependable revenue and profit stream that will flow through to a more consistent dividend policy.

Recently, assets under management in Morgan Stanley's wealth management division surpassed $2 trillion and this division is expected to continue to keep growing because of its focus on high net worth clients.

High Net Worth Clients

Morgan Stanley's Wealth Management division has increased its profitability by focusing on high net worth individuals and families. This focus allows Morgan Stanley to trim its roster of advisors while increasing assets. A recipe for increased profitability.

Morgan Stanley is already the leading wealth manager in the U.S. based on assets under management for high net worth individuals and families. This market segment, both domestic and globally, is expected to keep growing.

From Mckinsey's 2014 report on the wealth management industry.

- Despite slower global economic growth, the number of millionaires is expected to rise by 7.1 percent by 2018 to more than 18 million.
- By 2018, total HNW assets are expected to rise by 49 percent to USD 76 trillion. We expect Asia (excluding Japan) to create about USD 9 trillion in net new millionaire wealth.

As the leading high net worth wealth manager in the U.S., Morgan Stanley has the brand recognition, the network, and the expertise to serve this very profitable and growing segment. Morgan Stanley's leading wealth management attributes in the U.S. also offers Morgan Stanley a great opportunity to grow globally.

Lending

Morgan Stanley's focus and expertise on high net worth households allows it to add profitable ancillary services. Like lending.

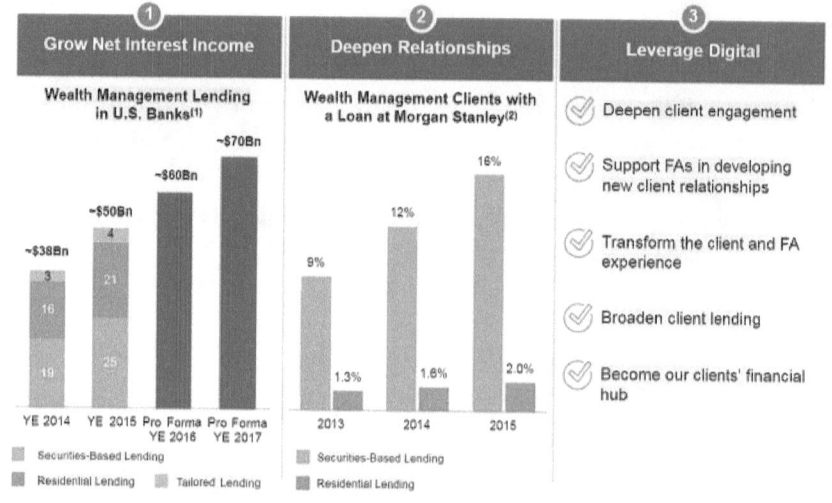

1 Grow Net Interest Income	**2** Deepen Relationships	**3** Leverage Digital

High net worth households come with an array of assets. And a lot of those assets are illiquid and hard to lend against in the traditional way. Through the existing relationship with their high net worth client Morgan Stanley is willing to lend against those assets. If interest rates rise Morgan Stanley's net interest margin, lending profitability, will rise too.

Increased Capital Return to Shareholders

As a result of the 2008 financial crisis, Morgan Stanley has to submit a capital return plan to the Federal Reserve for approval. Before approving a capital return plan the Federal Reserve is making sure Morgan Stanley is well capitalized and reserved against future potential losses.

The current requirement for Common Equity Tier 1 Ratio is 6.5%. Morgan Stanley's Common Equity Tier 1 Ratio currently stands at 15.8% well above current requirements. This even exceeds the Total Minimum Regulatory Capital Ratio of 9.375%.

Morgan Stanley is more than well reserved. It has excess capital in reserve and we expect the company to return this excess capital to shareholders through increased dividends and share buybacks.

Project Streamline

The other big opportunity for Morgan Stanley is large cost reductions. The company is currently initiating a large technology overhaul to reduce costs and streamline operations. Hence the name "Project Streamline".

Project Streamline: $1Bn Expense Reduction Through 2017

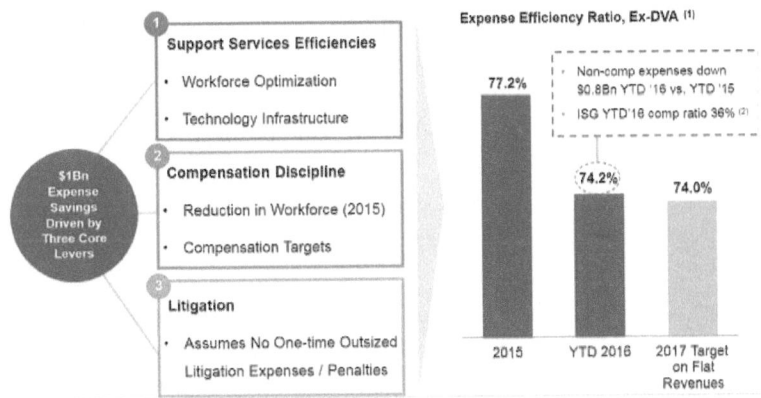

Reducing costs is a large component of increasing Morgan Stanley's efficiency ratio. The lower the ratio the better because it shows increasing profitability.

Pre-Mortem (Potential Risks to our Thesis)

DOL Fiduciary Rule

The big news in the financial advice industry has been the announcement of the new Fiduciary Rule by the Department of Labor. A financial advisor that is a fiduciary, like American Money Management, works with and acts in the best interest of their clients. Any financial advisor who isn't a fiduciary, someone who sells securities, insurance, or other financial products and earns a commission on them operates under the suitability rule. The product they sold to you has to be suitable to your needs.

It may sound like a minor difference but it has huge ramifications for your portfolio. The broker could sell you investment products that pay them a large commission but do not serve your long-term best interest and it would be OK if that product was "suitable" to your situation.

This isn't right.

The Department of Labor's new rule states that any person that advises on retirement accounts has to operate as a Fiduciary. This essentially ends the use of commissioned products in retirement accounts. Why sell them if you can't get paid on them?

A broker advising on retirement accounts can still sell commissioned products but they have to get consent from the client and maintain more paperwork to ensure that they are in compliance with the new rule. Some of the large brokerages are switching to a fee only model citing the regulatory burden. Others, like Morgan Stanley, will still allow its advisors to sell commissioned products in retirement accounts.

Morgan Stanley will also have the fee-only models. The continued selling of commissioned products in retirement accounts under the new Fiduciary Rule increases the chances for more lawsuits. It potentially puts Morgan Stanley at a competitive disadvantage to firms that offer fee-only advice.

This was written before the outcome of the 2016 Presidential election. It is a distinct possibility that the DOL Fiduciary rule will not go through with Trump winning the Presidency.

American Money Management

We would like to think that American Money Management LLC is a direct threat to Morgan Stanley but it is the collection of firms like us: boutique fee-only wealth managers. Also known as independent Registered Investment Advisors (RIAs). RIAs are the fastest growing segment in the wealth management industry and collectively manage well over a $1 trillion in assets

We think you understand the appeal; clear and fair pricing, high touch and individualized service, acting as fiduciaries.

Wealthy individuals and the mass affluent are moving their assets away from the large well-known brokerages to independent RIAs. Brokers are leaving too as they see the appeal in conflict free advice. The departing brokers are either taking their book of business to established RIAs or starting their own boutique firms. The large brokerage houses like Morgan Stanley have a lot more competition.

Increased Regulation & Capital Requirements

Morgan Stanley has to submit a capital return plan to the Federal Reserve each year before the company can increase its dividend and/or share buybacks. Right now Morgan Stanley has reserves in excess of its requirement. We think shareholders are going to be rewarded with a larger dividend and a larger share buyback over the next few years.

If those reserve requirements change then the potential capital returned to shareholders will be reduced. Higher reserve requirements lead to lower returns on equity. Morgan Stanley would like to use its capital to make more loans to its high net worth individuals and reinvest more in its business. Reserve capital cannot be put at risk and it cannot generate a return for the company. It is a drag on growth. Higher reserves would lower the returns Morgan Stanley can generate for its shareholders.

Conclusion

When we made our first purchase in Morgan Stanley near the end of September shares were trading around $31-32 per share. We valued the company at $40 per share. In the wake of the Presidential election and Donald Trump's victory financial companies have staged a strong rebound. The prevailing thought is that higher interest rates are coming when President-elect Donald Trump replaces Janet Yellen at the end of her term. Another belief is that recent increased regulation on financial companies will be rolled back. We think it is unlikely that Dodd-Frank will be repealed, but some of the regulations under its framework may be lessened. For Morgan Stanley specifically, we expect the Fiduciary Rule created under President Obama's administration, but not yet implemented, will not go through.

Less regulation and increased interest rates will drive our valuation of Morgan Stanley higher. Right now that environment doesn't exist and we have to wait and see if this scenario plays out under Trump's Presidency. We're maintaining our fair value of $40 per share for now and given recent strength we'll wait for a pullback to buy more.

Portfolio Update: Morgan Stanley (MS)

September 2018

We recently sold Morgan Stanley in the majority of accounts that held a position.*

We sold Morgan Stanley (MS) for two main reasons.

A Better Opportunity

When we say a "better opportunity" we mean a potential investment that is trading at a price well below our estimate of fair value and has the potential to grow its dividend at a higher rate than a current holding in the portfolio.

Along with selling Morgan Stanley, we initiated a position in Starbucks. We will explain our investment thesis in Starbucks further in a later Dividend Letter but recent U.S. operational issues have brought Starbucks stock price below our estimate of fair value. Starbucks current dividend yield is slightly higher than Morgan Stanley's. Given Starbucks' dominant market position, free cash flow generation, and international expansion opportunities we think Starbucks can grow its dividend at above-average rates for the foreseeable future.

Portfolio Management

We first started buying Morgan Stanley in client accounts back in September 2016. You can read our original investment thesis here. Then Donald Trump was elected President and the stocks of financial companies surged. Expectations of pro-business legislation, higher economic growth, more inflation, and a higher fed funds rate helped fuel the rise in financial stocks. Morgan Stanley quickly reached our estimate of fair value and has been trading around our fair value estimate ever since. Subsequently, our purchases of Morgan Stanley have stopped.

Last month we had the opportunity to initiate a position in Charles Schwab. With Wells Fargo, JP Morgan, BlackRock, Morgan Stanley, and now Charles Schwab our typical dividend strategy portfolio has become too concentrated in the financial sector. Morgan Stanley and Charles Schwab do compete with each other in multiple business divisions but we think Charles Schwab is better positioned for long-term secular growth.

We'll discuss this further in the next Dividend Letter. To reduce our financial stock exposure, we sold Morgan Stanley.

If you would like to discuss this further, feel free to contact us by email or by telephone at (858) 755-0909.

Sincerely,

Your Portfolio Management Team

Clients who have put a ceiling on their 2018 capital gains exposure may still hold all or a portion of their original position in MS so as to avoid additional realized taxable gains in 2018.

Disclaimer

The opinions expressed in "The AMM Dividend Letter" are those of Gabriel Wisdom, Michael Moore and Glenn Busch and do not necessarily reflect the opinions of American Money Management, LLC (AMM), an SEC registered investment advisor who serves as a portfolio manager to private accounts as well as to mutual funds. Clients of AMM, Mr. Wisdom, Mr. Moore, Mr. Busch, employees of AMM, and mutual funds AMM manages may buy or sell investments mentioned without prior notice. This book should not be considered investment advice and is for educational purposes only. The opinions expressed do not constitute a recommendation to buy or sell securities. Investing involves risks, and you should consult your own investment advisor, attorney, or accountant before investing in anything. Current stock quotes are obtained at http://finance.yahoo.com. Prices are as of the close of the market on the date for which the price is referenced.

About American Money Management

American Money Management is a Registered Investment Adviser located in Rancho Santa Fe, California. American Money Management may only transact business in those states or countries in which it is registered, or qualifies for an exemption or exclusion from registration requirements. For non-clients of the firm, American Money Management's web site is limited to the dissemination of general information pertaining to its investment advisory services.

Please contact Gabriel Wisdom or Michael Moore at **858-755-0909** to find out if we may conduct advisory business in the state or country where you reside. Accordingly, American Money Management does not, and will not, effect or attempt to effect transactions in securities, or the rendering of personalized investment advice for compensation, through this book. Any subsequent, direct communication with a prospective client shall be conducted by an American Money Management representative who is either registered or qualifies for an exemption or exclusion from registration in the state or country where the prospective client resides.

www.ingramcontent.com/pod-product-compliance
Lightning Source LLC
Chambersburg PA
CBHW021009180526
45163CB00005B/1940